You may renew this loan for a further period by phone, letter, personal visit or at www.kirklees.gov.uk/libraries provided that the book is not required by another reader

NO MORE THAN THR   /70

D1421946

'Most introductions to philosophy are either so simple as to be pointless or so high as to be incomprehensible. This book has bucked the trend and written one that actually might improve your brain. He's not afraid, either, to point out that many of the most pressing philosophical questions have now been solved, or at least discarded as irrelevant. A first point of call for anyone interested in the subject, and worth reading for those who've already spent some time wandering the labyrinth.' *Arena*

Also by Nicholas Fearn

Zeno and the Tortoise: How to Think Like a Philosopher

Philosophy

THE LATEST ANSWERS TO THE OLDEST QUESTIONS

nicholas fearn

Atlantic Books
London

First published in Great Britain in hardback in 2005 by
Atlantic Books, an imprint of Grove Atlantic Ltd.

This paperback edition published in Great Britain in 2006 by
Atlantic Books.

9 8 7 6 5 4 3 2 1

A CIP catalogue record for this book is available from
the British Library.

1 84354 068 1

Designed and typeset by Lindsay Nash
Printed in Great Britain by
Clays Ltd, St Ives plc

Atlantic Books
An imprint of Grove Atlantic Ltd
Ormond House
26–27 Boswell Street
London WC1N 3JZ

contents

acknowledgements

I am grateful to Tim Crane for helping me to plan this book and to Alan Thomas for his scrutiny of the end result. The task would not have been possible without the generosity of the following, whom I would like to thank for their time and advice: Ruth Barcan Marcus, Ned Block, Nick Bostrom, Tyler Burge, Simon Critchley, David Chalmers, Noam Chomsky, Patricia Churchland, Paul Churchland, Daniel Dennett, Cian Dorr, Hubert Dreyfus, Stuart Dreyfus, Jerry Fodor, Alvin Goldman, Christine Korsgaard, Colin McGinn, Hugh Mellor, Ruth Millikan, Martha Nussbaum, David Papineau, Alvin Plantinga, Hilary Putnam, Richard Rorty, Thomas Scanlon, John Searle, Peter Singer, Charles Taylor, Peter Van Inwagen, Timothy Williamson. I am also indebted to the late Donald Davidson and Bernard Williams. Thanks finally to my editors Toby Mundy, Alice Hunt and Bonnie Chiang.

preface

All the interests of my reason, speculative as well as
practical, combine in following three questions: (1) What
can I know? (2) What ought I to do? (3) What may I hope?

Immanuel Kant

There is room for words on subjects other than last words.
Indeed, the usual manner of presenting philosophical
work puzzles me. Works of philosophy are written as
though their authors believe them to be the absolutely
final word on their subject.

Robert Nozick

The Great philosophers such as Aristotle, Immanuel Kant and
Ludwig Wittgenstein achieved their status because they preferred
revolution to evolution. They would rather introduce new ideas and
systems than work with their predecessors' materials. The result was
that over two and half thousand years of philosophy, successive
thinkers covered their subjects' canvas with so many brushstrokes
that no discernible image remained. Only lately has a restoration
started to bear results. Layers have been removed and more naive
cleanings discarded. Old impressions have been revealed as the ideas
of ancient thinkers have gained new purchase, and contemporary
inks have refreshed the strongest lines. This has been made possible
by new techniques in the analysis of arguments, new ideas to test
them on and new raw material provided by the sciences.

Now is an ideal time to take an audit of Western philosophy. This book assesses the current state of the philosophical art, taking a wide view of what has been achieved in recent years in the most hotly contested areas, and examines the latest approaches to problems that were first tackled in the ancient world. In order to complete my audit, I decided to consult a cross section of the main players in the key debates from various parts of the world. My task was made easier in the end by the concentration of most of the finest philosophical minds in a single – if large – place, the United States. It was made harder by the advanced age of the interviewees, several of whom, including Robert Nozick and W. V. O. Quine, died before I could get to see them. Most of those who survived were amenable, though some were more amenable than others. Several, such as David Chalmers, Jerry Fodor and Colin McGinn welcomed me into their homes, while others such as Thomas Nagel and Alasdair MacIntyre were so suspicious of journalists that they refused to speak to me. Daniel Dennett and Tyler Burge kindly allowed me second drafts and follow-up questions, while Jacques Derrida telephoned me before sunrise to decline to help when I was in no fit state to argue.

In the end I was able to interview over thirty of the world's most prominent thinkers. After the first few meetings, I noticed that the conversation usually took the same direction. First they would inform me that, sadly, there had been little progress in philosophical understanding during their lifetime. Then they would begin a long exposition of evidence to the contrary. It seems that the typical modern philosopher is nothing if not modest. Philosophy has always suffered from excessive expectations, but if it is foolhardy to declare a final solution to any philosophical problem, it is equally rash to dismiss anything less as worthless. Over the past fifty years, revolution has gone out of fashion in the philosophical world. Answers have tended to come in a smaller size than those of the past – as, cynics would add, have the thinkers who proffer them. Even cynics, however, would admit that technical ability is at an all-time high. A decent graduate student in the subject today should be able to hold his own in a debate against any illustrious thinker from the ancient world. There are fewer gurus, fewer giants, but a greater division of labour in an increasingly fragmented and specialized field. On the face of it there is little agreement among these disparate schools. But the consensus is often stronger than it seems, for once a field has been more or less wrapped up, then, as the philosophers Cian Dorr and Daniel Dennett sometimes argue, the researchers who persist in working in it tend to be the eccentrics. For example, most scientists are satisfied that aliens have not been visiting the Earth in flying saucers recently, yet a survey of the specialist literature on 'alien abduction' shows that the vast majority of so-called 'experts' are firm believers in UFOs and little green men. This is because most scientists have better things to do than tackle questions that have already been settled within reasonable doubt.

Philosophy has entered a 'post-heroic' age. Contemporary philosophers hope to advance our understanding incrementally as they build on a distributed achievement – the work of over twenty-six thousand professionals worldwide according to the Philosophical Documentation Center – informed by the latest work in the rest of the humanities and sciences. The role of the genius has diminished, perhaps because of a dearth of such individuals in recent years, perhaps due to the time it takes to recognize them as such, but more likely because the discipline has learned from its imperialistic mistakes. One of these mistakes is overreach. At the beginning of the nineteenth century, the German philosopher Georg Hegel used his philosophical system to predict that there could be only seven planets in the solar system. Today, one hopes, philosophers have a better idea of what can and cannot be achieved by reasoned argument. Neither do philosophers find it necessary to turn their subject on its head in order to solve philosophical problems. There is no need for revolution when constant, steady progress is already being made.

Today's philosophers look back on at least five great revolutions in ideas. The first was the birth of reason as an instrument for divining truth in the fifth and sixth centuries BC, which comes to us through the surviving works of the Presocratic philosophers and the dialogues of Plato. Building upon the thoughts of his teacher, Socrates, Plato held our views to be correct or mistaken insofar as they corresponded with the otherworldly 'Forms' of Beauty, Goodness, Courage and the like. Plato held these templates to be objects in themselves – more real, in fact, than the objects that we find in the physical world, for they were perfect, pure, eternal and unchanging. He maintained that by employing reason properly we could come to see these truths and attain genuine knowledge with which to replace the mere 'opinion' with which we are normally satisfied. The only limit was the material we had to work with – for the physical world contains but inferior copies of the eternal truths.

In Königsberg in the eighteenth century, the second great revolution was effected when Immanuel Kant transferred the emphasis to the human subject. Everything we see and hear, everything the mind apprehends must, he thought, be shaped by the senses and the intellect for our comprehension. We can never behold the intrinsic nature of things as Plato dreamed. We can only ever know an anthropic version of God, Virtue and Beauty. In Kant's formulation, the more familiar we become with the capabilities of our own minds, the closer we approach true knowledge. We can only understand the limits of our world by examining the limits of human thought.

The third great revolution took place at around the same time in Britain. John Locke and David Hume had worked the scientific methodology of their seventeenth-century predecessor Francis Bacon into a philosophical system known as 'empiricism'. According to the empiricists, we could only know that which was within our experience. Reason alone could unearth nothing new, but merely rearticulate knowledge already furnished by the senses.

In the nineteenth century, a further revolution occurred when the German thinker Georg Hegel initiated the study of what Man may become rather than simply what he is, citing the historical forces that trump reason in the creation of new ideas and modes of living. His 'dialectic' traced the clash of opposing movements to chart 'the progress in the consciousness of liberty', and defined the state that embodied this development as 'the march of God through the world'. Where Hegel attacked reason from above, his fellow countryman Friedrich Nietzsche undercut it with an appeal to motive. He argued that values were rendered true by the individual's 'Will to Power' rather than any recourse to evidence and observation. At a stroke, Nietzsche provided the foundation for the anti-philosophy known as 'postmodernism' that remains so popular in humanities departments.

By the early twentieth century, the limits were drawn tighter as philosophers such as the Austrian Ludwig Wittgenstein created a fifth revolution by proposing that the boundaries of thought were delineated by the limits of the language in which it was conducted. The standards for assessing truth resided neither in the heavens nor in the confines of the mind, but in the grammar of public practice. Where philosophers imagined that they were examining the nature of things, all they were really doing, Wittgenstein and his followers argued, were taking words out of their context. The proper objects of study were, for Plato, semi-divine entities and, for Kant, the structures of consciousness. Now, 'analytic' philosophers were reduced to analysing the grunts and bodily jerks that human beings use to communicate. For excitement, they could hunt down and extinguish vestiges of metaphysical thinking and pronounce problems 'dissolved'. For example, the English philosopher Gilbert Ryle argued that the question of where to locate the conscious self was a 'category mistake' of the kind made by someone who visits the colleges of Oxford and asks where the 'university' is, or watches a procession of battalions and regiments and asks when the 'army' will be marching past.

Western thinkers today are informed by all these shifts, but one in particular has captured their imagination in recent years: the empiricist promise of a 'scientific' philosophy. Bertrand Russell once compared the branches of human knowledge to a filing cabinet, in which the material discussed by philosophers was found in the compartment marked 'Don't Know'. Once we have found out enough about a given subject to approach its questions in a systematic way, the contents are moved into a new compartment with a new title, be it 'Physics', 'Psychology' or 'Economics'. This is a fair description of the history of philosophy, which has periodically resulted in new disciplines, new sciences. It also explains the illusion that philosophy never achieves anything. Philosophers never get the credit for their successes, for once real progress has been made on a problem it is taken out of their hands and given to its new custodians. Sir Isaac Newton wrote the *Principia* and Adam Smith *The Wealth of Nations* as philosophers, but they are now remembered respectively as a physicist and an economist. The contemporary thinker Noam Chomsky is described as a philosopher as well as the founder of linguistics, but the former half of his title will one day be dropped from encyclopedias.

This fate has led to the recent proposition that, since philosophy seems to succeed where it has spun off new sciences, the whole subject should be made into a science. Such a belief in 'scientism' is tantamount to a small boy asking his father why, if the soldiers of the SAS are so deadly, the generals don't turn the entire army into one big SAS. Neither knowledge nor armies work in this way. Demanding that thought be conducted always and only according to rigorous scientific principles would mean that some subjects – those about which we know least – would never be tackled, and no new disciplines would develop. However, the issue is about more than the best way to nurture ideas, since that assumes that it is the destiny of every useful method of enquiry to become a scientific one. The difference between philosophy and science is often a matter of timing rather than a division of subject matter. Sometimes philosophy terminates in science. Very occasionally, it solves a problem without giving birth to a new discipline and, sometimes, this is because the problem has been dissolved rather than solved. The chapters that follow contain a mixture of these outcomes.

Some contemporary thinkers find the claims of physics and biology an unwelcome trespass on their territory and mock the 'science envy' of their colleagues who linger outside laboratory doors, ready to rush into print the philosophical repercussions of the latest discovery. There is a widespread belief that philosophy, alone among the arts and sciences, must be democratic. While few of us entertain personal theories of fluid dynamics or pretend that we can write like

Hemingway, it is commonly believed that anyone can grasp philosophical insights. Moreover, it is not just that anyone can be so gifted, but that anyone at any time in the past could have enjoyed the same benefits. The world, which shows so little fairness in everything else, is supposed to be inherently just and equitable when it comes to knowledge and understanding of the most profound truths. It is imagined that answers can be picked by anyone like apples. This has proved to be wishful thinking. Some truths lie within easy reach on the lower boughs, but others have proved unattainable without the invention of ladders. Though it is harsh to imagine the philosophers of past generations – who were often great geniuses – working their entire lives without hope of ever alighting on the truth, this is exactly what many of them were doing. Perhaps these thinkers produced faulty theories and inconclusive arguments because they did not think hard or carefully enough. But the problem is more simple than this: they did not have the right equipment to find what they were looking for, because such equipment did not exist.

This equipment takes many forms: a particular breed of argument or a logical device, a mechanical aid such as a brain scanner or a photograph of the Earth from space. No matter how good our eyesight, we were never going to understand the stars, or work out that those pinpricks of light in the night sky were what we now understand to be stars, by squinting at them. The telescope, on the other hand, enabled even those with relatively poor eyesight to behold the planets. No doubt there are many problems that are insoluble today because we lack the equipment that might become available to our descendants. It is not so much science that is important in discovering the truth, but technology in one form or another. Part of the reason for the past failures of philosophy is the same as that for the failure of early flying machines and efforts to cure diseases: the means were not in place. Though philosophy would seem to float free of matters of empirical facts, much of it is dependent upon them, and not all solutions are equally accessible to all peoples at all times, let alone all individuals. This should be a cause for relief, for it demonstrates that our enquiries concern mind-independent truths as opposed to a navel-gazing study of our own selves.

The hope for a 'democratic' philosophy also springs from the Ancient Greek ideal of Truth as mathematical in form. The truths of philosophy were to mimic the truths of number in being derivable from first principles. This was natural for what were assumed to be necessary truths. But it seems that philosophical truths, insofar as we can speak of them, can be accidental, written in the sands rather than the stars. By this yardstick, the history of philosophy has always been a record of disappointment. As the discipline spawns new sciences, these offspring are more comfortable than their parent with the arbitrariness of the laws governing their discoveries. Each leaves a lacuna in a womb that fails to collapse with the birth of the child.

Although a new science may solve the problems that preceded it when philosophers were doing all the work, there has always seemed to be something missing, as if the solution wasn't quite what was intended, or wasn't for exactly the problem in mind. Studying the results can be like catching a stage conjurer's sleight of hand: 'You've hidden the card in your sleeve – that's not *real* magic at all!' One area of philosophy that has been particularly blighted by this thinking is the question of what constitutes moral action. The English philosopher G. E. Moore was led to deem morality an unanalysable property by what he called the 'Naturalistic Fallacy'. He observed that once we identify a motive for an act – even a supposedly ethical one – it ceases to be moral: 'You helped her out of pleasure (or charity, or duty, or whatever) – *morality* had nothing to do with it!' If these are our expectations, it is not surprising that they get frustrated.

We look for philosophical answers to philosophical problems, but these answers may not match the mood of the question if the aim is to remove a mystery. The sense of drama that attends perplexity usually evaporates upon its resolution. This is a turn-off for those individuals drawn to philosophy for a more adult form of escapism than stories of ghosts, goblins and UFOs. Did alien visitors build the pyramids? No, but computers might be able to think. For some, the works of philosophers such as Hilary Putnam, Richard Rorty and Daniel Dennett are a natural progression from Erik Von Daniken's *Chariots of the Gods.* Those who come to philosophy via disillusionment with religion are liable to find themselves even more disappointed. But should they complain that the solutions provided by their new field lack the security of the old – that, for example, without God there is ultimately no sense in morality – then one is entitled to ask how exactly we were supposed to have morality *with* God.

Another common route into the subject, shared by Wittgenstein and Gottfried Leibniz among others, has been mathematical studies. Such a background might prepare one better to accept the peculiar rewards of philosophical research and to share the attitude expressed by the physicist Richard Feynman:

> I have a friend who's an artist, and he has sometimes taken a view which I don't agree with very well. He'll hold up a flower and say, 'Look how beautiful it is,' and I'll agree. And he says, 'You see, I as an artist can see how beautiful this is, but you, as a scientist, take

this all apart and it becomes a dull thing.' And I think he's kind of nutty. First of all, the beauty that he sees is available to other people and to me, too, I believe, although I might not be quite as refined aesthetically as he is. I can appreciate the beauty of a flower, and at the same time I see much more about the flower than he sees. I could imagine the cells in there, the complicated actions inside which also have a beauty. It's not just beauty at this dimension of one centimetre: there is also beauty at a smaller dimension, the inner structure … also the processes. The fact that the colours in the flower are evolved in order to attract insects to pollinate it is interesting – it means that insects can see the colour. It adds a question – does this aesthetic sense also exist in the lower forms? Or why is it aesthetic? There are all kinds of interesting questions which a science knowledge only adds to the excitement and mystery and awe of a flower.[1]

Those who do not share Feynman's attitude are nostalgic not for the explanatory power of discredited religious answers (for often they had no such power), but for a supposed mystical experience that could reduce them to silence. In engaging the public, modern philosophy's real problem is not an envy of science, but a hunger for magic.

part one

who am I?

1
the problem of the self

For my part, when I enter most intimately into what I call myself, I always stumble on some particular perception or other, of heat or cold, light or shade, love or hatred, pain or pleasure. I can never catch myself at any time without a perception, and never can observe anything but the perception.

David Hume

The human body is the best picture of the human soul.

Ludwig Wittgenstein

You enter the brain through the eye, march up the optic nerve, round and round the cortex, looking behind every neuron, and then, before you know it, you emerge into daylight on the spike of a motor nerve impulse, scratching your head and wondering where the self is.

Daniel Dennett

After his death in 1683, Roger Williams, the founder of the Rhode Island colony, was buried beneath a young apple tree in his garden, and lay there until one day in 1936 when the local government decided to exhume his remains and place them in a monument to mark the state's tercentenary. However, when the coffin was opened, what the gravediggers found was not Williams's body. Some time in the preceding 253 years, a root from the apple tree had penetrated the casket and slowly absorbed the nutrients from the bones, leaving only fragments. In the process, the root had grown into the exact shape of the skeleton – entering through the skull, proceeding down the spine and parting to form two legs. Generations of schoolchildren had eaten fruit from the tree and were said to have become as independently minded as Williams as a result.

This story highlights a problem the Christian God would face should He decide to effect Judgement Day by reassembling the matter that once composed the bodies of the faithful. If He used the original atoms, ownership disputes would arise wherever the same matter had been part of different individuals' bodies at different times. One might assume that cannibals would lose out to the Christians they consumed, but the Almighty would surely face a tougher decision when considering the claims of unsuspecting Rhode Island schoolchildren after Roger Williams's remains entered the food chain. Perhaps God could circumvent the problem by creating a substitute for any contested matter so that there would be enough to go around. But then there would be a question of how much cosmic Polyfilla He could use without making someone a different person. There would be no sense in punishing or rewarding someone who was only a simulacrum of the perpetrator.

One does not have to wait for Judgement Day for this question to arise, as the matter from which our bodies are composed is almost completely replenished between birth and death. If the body is to be the seat of the soul, we should be aware that the only parts of it that remain with us throughout our lives are the ova of women and the lenses of the eyes. While eyes may be thought to be the window to the soul, one would hope that the soul is more than a few cubic millimetres of transparent jelly. As for the ova, this would leave us puzzling over where the souls of men reside. However, despite our constantly changing physical make-up, most of us feel that we are the same person as the child in our parents' photo album, and feel confident that we will retain this identity as the senior citizens we will eventually become. Neither does one have to wait for God to give a moral dimension to the problem of personal identity. The issue of whether the old man is the same person as the younger bears on how deeply we should feel guilt and pride in our youth; it determines how we should think of our memories. It also impinges on how we should behave towards the people we will become, whether giving up smoking is a matter of long-term self-interest or of altruism towards a quite different self. Perhaps, most importantly, our answer to the problem of personal identity determines whether any of us has a future at all, whether after death or even before it.

In 1785, the Scottish philosopher Thomas Reid wrote: 'Whatever this self may be, it is something which thinks, and deliberates and resolves, and acts, and suffers. I am not thought, I am not action, I am not feeling; I am something that thinks, and acts, and suffers.'[1] This proviso meant that anything within one's experience – anything in the world that we could come to know or discover – would be disqualified from claiming the title of 'oneself'. Hence it has been assumed that the self would be an extra-worldly kind of entity, an ego or soul or some unitary object that, if only we could track it, would answer the question of personal identity: 'Where the ego goes, I go.' As Reid's fellow countryman David Hume noted, we cannot observe an ego through introspection. We alight only on our perceptions and emotions, never on the possessor of these qualities. Philosophers have sought to overcome this blind spot by looking sideways at one's journey through life. What the self is in the present could best be discerned, it was thought, by examining what persists from one year to another across various bodily and psychological changes. Thus a large part of philosophers' work on the subject has been a kind of 'intuition mining', where we imagine changes in our mental and physical make-up and ask whether we would *feel* that personal identity had been preserved. Intuition is not usually given such a starring role in philosophy, but when it comes to personal identity we have only our own word to go on, since no such thing as a distinct self seems to appear in Nature's inventory alongside bodies, brains and personalities.

It is tempting to look beyond Nature for something outside our worldly existence, but this cannot solve the problem of personal identity. If there were a soul – a transcendent ego that owned one's experiences – then we could never know whether it stayed in the same place or wandered, lived or died. Everything that we can be aware of is an experience, and this ego – being the supposed recipient of all one's experiences – could never appear as one of them. Since our memories are among our experiences, these would be left behind by a departing ego. So one's ego might have been attached to a different set of experiences yesterday, or to a different body tomorrow, and we would be none the wiser. Two people might even be swapping egos a hundred times a second without ever being aware of it. They would have no way of noticing, because a change of egos is a change of something outside their experiences. To the mystically inclined, a world of untethered egos, each devoid of traits and indistinguishable from the next, might indicate a monism in which all of us are part of one great universal soul. However, it needs to be asked what exactly constitutes 'us' here, since it does not include our memories, personalities, bodies, brains or emotions – these mundane characteristics remain as separate from one another as ever, each housed in an individual man or woman. Any universal ego would seem to be a oneness of nothing. The more we wish to gain immortality by divesting ourselves of earthly trappings such as physicality, memories and the like, the more we reduce ourselves to nothing at all – and, to quote the American children's author Norton Juster, doing nothing is hardly worth the effort.

According to Ancient Greek legend, after the hero Theseus had slain the Minotaur in Crete, his ship was taken on an annual voyage of thanks to the island of Delos. Over the years, the beams of the vessel rotted away one by one and were gradually replaced until, eventually, none of the original timbers remained. The ship still looked like the one Theseus had commanded, but we might wonder whether it was now *the very same* ship. Since there is continuity from one stage of the ship's life to the next, we might decide that the later model is indeed the same ship as that which first set sail for Crete. But now suppose that the discarded planks had been collected and used to construct a new vessel to the original design. There would now be two rivals with claims to the identity of the Ship of Theseus, and the puzzle is that we feel unable to give a verdict even though we seem to know everything about the two candidates. Since we know all the relevant facts about the case, our ignorance must pertain instead to the concepts we are applying to it. There seems to be something inconsistent in the notion that identity is some special, further fact outside the ordinary properties of objects. George Washington's axe is supposedly on display in a museum somewhere in the United States. It is labelled as the very axe that chopped down the famous cherry tree, although the notes for visitors also mention that both the handle and the blade have since been replaced. In the absence of a discrete relation called 'identity', any labelling seems arbitrary. However, when it comes to ourselves we are unwilling to accept that identity might be purely a matter of labelling. We are left wondering whether our real identity belongs to the self we now inhabit or whether that identity is more truly represented by the greyed, creaking ghost ship of one's younger self.

The task of storing the discarded timbers of our lives is performed in our memories. In his 1690 work *An Essay Concerning Human Understanding*, the English philosopher John Locke proposed that the essential kernel of each human being is their consciousness, their self-awareness. Locke was aware of how counter-intuitive it seemed that something so nebulous – as opposed to a physical body or even an ethereal soul – could persist through time, since it was only marginally a 'thing' at all. He argued that self-awareness was not just a consciousness of the present, but also of the past, given to us in memory. To be the same person as your younger self was to be able to remember being that child, with the sequence of memories providing a psychological thread through one's lifetime.

Memory is imperfect and I may suffer lapses or blanks in my mental record without thereby being a different person at any time. Amnesia is not equivalent to death, we like to think. But perhaps it is quite close to it. Perhaps we have been kept awake at night by the thought that in the morning we will remember neither our final waking thoughts nor the fact that this prospect concerned us. The advanced stages of Alzheimer's disease debilitate the memory so severely that not only can someone forget their keys, they can also forget what keys are for. Sufferers have been known to attack the spouses they do not recognize, believing them to be intruders in their home. When someone has forgotten all their friends and family, their past and even their name, it can seem that they have indeed become a different person – if they can still be called a person. Alzheimer's disease is a powerful argument against life after death, because if you can be dead when you are alive then you can certainly be dead when you are dead.

In searching for a self we look for something over and above our attributes, but we do not usually think this way about ordinary objects. For example, I believe that my favourite armchair persists through time without imagining it to have a chair-soul or a chair-ego that possesses its traits. It has characteristics such as being three feet high at the seat, padded with foam and covered with green cloth, but there is no chair over and above these characteristics. If we took away the foam and the seat and the cloth and so on, we would not be left with a naked chair, as if objects were ghostly coat hangers upon which traits are hung. Yet this is precisely what we often imagine to be true in the case of persons. Abandoning this delusion draws a sharp difference between our situation and that of Thomas Reid's day. When an immaterial soul was presumed to exist and there was rarely any doubt that a unitary self existed, personal characteristics were the footprints of the soul – indicators of personal identity, signs that pointed towards the self. Today, on the other hand, one's traits are taken to *be* one's self, as there is nowhere else to find the latter that is recognized by science. The question now is which particular traits are the most significant – and whether they can give us what we are looking for.

The late English philosopher Sir Bernard Williams argued that we identify more closely with our bodies than our minds. I was lucky enough to meet Williams before he died in June 2003, aged seventy-three, following a long struggle against cancer. He held forth on the gamut of philosophical issues in a way that made him the exemplar of the modern thinker. Erudite and candid, Williams moved within the mainstream of his discipline and changed it significantly at several junctures without overturning the intellectual order. He was born in Westcliff, Essex, and was introduced to philosophy as a student at Balliol College, Oxford. He mastered the subject so quickly that some of his fellow undergraduates neglected to turn up for tutorials in order to attend lessons from Williams in the junior common room instead. After finishing his studies he spent what he regarded as the happiest years of his life on national service as a Spitfire pilot in Canada. He was brought into political work by his first wife, the MP Shirley Williams, and for his efforts in moral philosophy he was appointed to government commissions on gambling, drugs and pornography.

To test our intuitions about the self, Williams concocts an imaginary scenario in which we are at the mercy of a mad scientist who has a programme of physical torture scheduled for the following day.[2] He asks whether we would feel any less frightened if the scientist promised to wipe our memory clean before setting to work with the red-hot pliers. In a moment of generosity, he offers to replace our old memories with those of a completely different person – say, Napoleon. If memory is where selfhood lies, then we would have nothing to fear from the new day, as it would be 'Napoleon' who was going to suffer and not us. However, most of us would find little comfort in the scientist's sweetener. Indeed, it may even seem worse to suffer the double indignity of torture *and* amnesia, although the great commander's iron resolve and forbearance would doubtless come in handy during the ordeal. Neither would it bring any comfort if my persecutor were to take a second victim and replace his memories and the rest of his personality with mine. If I had to decide, on purely selfish grounds, who was to be tortured and who was to be given £10,000 and set free, I would have no trouble in choosing to give the cash to 'Napoleon'.

However, some futurists not only claim to prefer the opposite, but actually imagine paying good money for such a memory transferral. In *The Age of Spiritual Machines*, Ray Kurzweil speculates that one day we will be able to download our consciousness into computers, and live in better virtual worlds perhaps, or live forever. This will involve upgrading the 'hardware' on which the 'software' of your self runs. 'Today,' writes Kurzweil, 'our software cannot grow. It is stuck in a brain of a mere 100 trillion connections and synapses. But when the hardware is trillions of times more capable, there is no reason for our minds to stay so small. They can and will grow.' As better, faster, more capacious artificial brains come on to the market, the fragile, limited, messy neurons of the biological brains we grew up with will begin to look passé. More and more of us will make the switch to circuitry, and then our immortality will be 'a matter of being sufficiently careful to make frequent backups. If we're careless about this, we'll have to load an old backup copy and be doomed to repeat our recent past.'[3]

We might imagine a punter plugging his brain into a computer, then the husk of his body collapsing in a heap and finally his face appearing on the monitor. However, this is not what would happen. Nothing would jump from his brain into the machine. All that occurs is copying, just as, when you download a file from the Internet, the original file does not get sucked out of its home-server and rehoused in your PC. There is no reason why the process should not leave you as you are – conscious and in the same old body – while creating a confused silicon doppelgänger. And if the original 'you' is *not* left intact, then it would seem that the 'downloading' process is fatal. The same flaw is present in the famous 'transporter' machines in *Star Trek*, which supposedly take a traveller apart atom by atom and create them anew in a different location. Captain Kirk commits an elaborate form of suicide every time Scotty beams him up. One is able to think differently only by disregarding common notions of identity.

The Swedish philosopher Nick Bostrom is only too eager to rid us of such ideas. His working time is spent exploring what he described to me over the telephone as our 'trans-human' future, asking what life will be like when technology has transformed our bodies and minds. He insisted to me that, as long as the technology had been shown to work reliably, he would be happy to be uploaded into a computer while his original physical form was destroyed, if this meant that he would enjoy a better life as an upload. And, as for a process that would leave his original body intact:

> Our expectation about what will happen is a psychological state that hasn't evolved to cope with those kinds of cases. On another level we have no uncertainty at all – in that we know that there will be copying and that there will be precisely two candidates afterwards, one in the computer and one in the physical world. I think the least distortion between the two levels is caused by mapping the outcomes to probabilities. Suppose, for example, that we know tomorrow we are to be bifurcated into two selves with equal claim to identity with my present self, and that one of these selves will be tortured horribly. I think I should feel the same as if there was to be no bifurcation but a 50 per cent chance that I was going to suffer the same experience tomorrow.

One wonders whether distance would be an issue in the transfers of selfhood that Bostrom has in mind, for there is also the problem of how to distinguish between intentional and unintentional copying. Imagine, for example, being atomized in an industrial accident while, in another galaxy, a group of alien scientists unintentionally create a computer configuration that corresponds to your brain patterns, just like the one that scientists on earth might have created on purpose. Presumably, one would not expect to wake up in the Andromeda galaxy in this instance. Neither would Bostrom. For him, the important difference is that there is no causal connection between his original self and the aliens' creation. As he wrote to me: 'The accidental copy will not be in any way affected by what I do, so it makes little sense to adjust my attitudes and feelings to take account of its existence.' On the face of it this seems an odd way of talking about identity, because it is the fate of a particular self that is at issue rather than anyone's feelings or expectations. Perhaps the original individual can influence what happens to a planned copy after his body has been destroyed, whereas he cannot influence one created by accident, but this has no bearing on what each copy is like intrinsically. The history of each is very different for sure, but we want identity to be more than just a story. Nonetheless, a story is all we are going to get once selfhood is revealed to be a matter of narratives and relations rather than objects and traits.

These thought experiments show that while memory, personality, emotions and other psychological traits might be indicative of personal identity, they are not constitutive of it. Before the intervention of Bernard Williams, we may have felt unsure whether psychological alterations would cause us to become a truly different person or the same person with different characteristics. But the prospect of physical torture sharpens the mind. When the chips are down and the pliers are hot, we think of ourselves as bodies, or at least as brains. The brain, rather than the body as a whole, is today the last refuge of the self. If brain transplants are ever perfected, then my body, like my present car, might one day belong to someone else. But there is no chance that my *brain* could belong to someone else. I could give someone my kidney, or heart or lungs, but I could not give him my brain without turning him into me, albeit with a different body.

The brain, however, can be changed – its pathways altered, its cells damaged – without us losing our selfhood. Brains have two hemispheres, and removing one of them is the correct surgical procedure for treating certain forms of brain tumour. People can survive this process with their identity intact, although they may suffer disabilities such as loss of speech. Many patients make a good recovery as their remaining brain hemisphere relearns the skills that were lost. If I undergo such radical surgery either 'I' will survive it or 'I' won't survive. It does not seem possible that I should only partially survive, since if any part survives then the operation is a success as far as I am concerned. If 1 per cent of my brain were removed, I should obviously expect to wake up and still be me. If 100 per cent were destroyed and replaced I should certainly expect not to and will feel doomed. If the proportion is 50 per cent I will feel unsure and worried, and pray that I wake up with a sore scalp and a lighter head. But it is not as if there is a 'me', a self, hanging around in the air to inhabit or not inhabit one of these possibilities. Whoever is lying there on the operating table is going to wake up, and he will be whoever he is. There would be no difference between the patient's waking up and being 'me' and his waking up and being someone else. All there is to know concerns the proportions of tissue involved and the results as reported by the patient afterwards. Barring the supernatural, there are just no extra facts that remain to be discovered. There might be a critical level of replacement which settles the question, but we cannot assume this any more than we can assume that there is a crucial grain of sand that turns a pile into a heap or a final hair follicle which, once gone, leaves a 'thinning' man 'bald'.

Suppose we now try to imagine what would happen if the other hemisphere of the brain were saved and transplanted into a new body. Since the two hemispheres are taken to be identical, which body should I expect to wake up in? I cannot wake up in both bodies, as I cannot be two people at once. There seems to be no reason for me to wake up in body A rather than body B, or vice versa, which leads to the suspicion that we can really expect to wake up in neither body. The problem is that we have run out of facts. Once we have full descriptions of the initial patient and the two survivors, we know everything about the case. We know where the brain parts have gone and we know where the bodies have gone. But there are no further facts left that we can look to in order to settle the question of whether body A will be 'me'. In looking for 'me' we can look only for my components and attributes, and, if knowing all there is to know about these factors cannot settle our question, then the question is an empty one.

The dissolution of the paradox is not comforting when it comes to our own lives. We are disposed to conclude that division is tantamount to death. But if we accept this, then we must revise our expectations in the earlier case, where only one hemisphere of the brain survives. This too must count as death, because the relationship between what wakes up and what fell asleep cannot be affected by a third party, even an extra brain hemisphere that survives. Whatever survives the operation that destroys half my brain, then, will not be me (no matter how much whoever wakes up protests that he is me). And yet, asks the British philosopher Derek Parfit: 'How could I fail to survive if the other half of my brain was also success- fully transplanted? How could a double success be a failure?'[4] To think in this way, he argues, is to make the mistake once again of assuming that there is something important that we do not know – some further factor in the nature of the self akin to a soul that could preserve our identity. Rejecting this assumption, Parfit argues that to view division as demise is arbitrary, as my surviving the operation and my not surviving are not two genuinely different possibilities, either of which might be true. Survival and death here are 'merely two different descriptions of the same outcome'.[5] He suggests that we regard division rather like a drug that doubles your lifespan – only the extra years are to run concurrently.

We have to remember that the operation is effectively performed on all of us several times over the course of our lives – during child- hood when neural tissue is being formed, as well as later when it degenerates. It can look as though we will cease to exist long before our deaths. Were there such a unity as a soul at the heart of us, we might imagine it squeezing over into the left hemisphere of the brain as the right hemisphere is cut away, as if jumping from plank to plank as successive beams of Theseus' ship are replaced. But there is no evi- dence that any such thing takes place in nature. The personal identity debate shows just what happens when we dispense with the soul. For Parfit, the consequences are liberating. He writes that when he thought his existence a fact distinct from his physical and psycho- logical continuity, he seemed 'imprisoned' in himself. 'My life seemed like a glass tunnel, through which I was moving faster every year, and at the end of which there was darkness.'[6] However:

> When I changed my view, the walls of my glass tunnel disappeared. I now live in the open air. There is still a difference between my life and the lives of other people. But the difference is less. Other people are closer. I am less concerned about the rest of my own life, and more concerned about the lives of others.[7]

Another response might be to dwell on how the fleeting status of human existence has been accentuated. Not only are human beings continually coming into being and passing away, but they are even doing this on countless occasions within a single lifetime. We are, it seems, a flicker within a flicker.

2
free will and fate

> A strict belief in fate is the worst kind of slavery; on the
> other hand there is comfort in the thought that God will be
> moved by our prayers.
>
> *Epicurus*

> We want our beliefs to be caused by the relevant facts in
> the world – as this will give us knowledge and help us to
> act successfully – yet we are not as eager for our actions
> to be caused by those facts, even where the price is the
> failure to attain our goals.
>
> *Robert Nozick*

In 1924, two teenagers stood trial in Cook County, Illinois, for the murder of fourteen-year-old Bobby Franks. It was the case that inspired Alfred Hitchcock's *Rope*, and the Orson Welles movie *Compulsion* (directed by Richard Fleischer). Franks had known his killers – both brilliant students from wealthy Chicago families. Eighteen-year-old Richard Loeb was the son of a retired Sears and Roebuck vice-president and had been the youngest-ever graduate of the University of Michigan, while his nineteen-year-old lover, Nathan Leopold Jr, was the son of a packaging magnate and already one of America's leading authorities on ornithology. Leopold had been drawn to the work of the late nineteenth-century German philosopher Friedrich Nietzsche, and in particular his idea that exceptional men were above the moral norms that bound the majority. Leopold considered Loeb an example of Nietzsche's *Übermensch*, or 'Superman', and was willing to help him commit the 'perfect' crime in order to demonstrate their contempt for society. The pair abducted Loeb's distant cousin, Bobby Franks, on his way home from school one afternoon in May, inviting him into the car they had hired for the occasion, attacking him with a chisel and finally suffocating him. After disfiguring the body and hiding it in a drainage channel, they sent a ransom note to the Franks family demanding $10,000 in unmarked bills. However, Bobby Franks's body was discovered and identified before the money was delivered. The investigators found an unusual pair of spectacles at the scene, and the prescription was traced to Nathan Leopold.

At the trial, the celebrated lawyer Clarence Darrow made an unusual plea for clemency on behalf of his clients, who had both pleaded guilty:

> To believe that any boy is responsible for himself or his early
> training is an absurdity ... If his failing came from his heredity, I do
> not know where or how. None of us are bred perfect and pure; and
> the colour of our hair, the colour of our eyes, our stature, the
> weight and fineness of our brain, and everything about us could,
> with full knowledge, be traced with absolute certainty to
> somewhere. If we had the pedigree it could be traced just the same
> in a boy as it could in a dog ... If it did not come that way, then ...
> if he had been understood, if he had been trained as he should have
> been it would not have happened. If there is responsibility
> anywhere, it is back of him; somewhere in the infinite number of
> his ancestors, or in his surroundings, or in both. And I submit,
> Your Honour, that under every principle of ... right, and of law, he
> should not be made responsible for the acts of someone else ...

Is Dickey Loeb to blame because out of the infinite forces that conspired to form him, the infinite forces that were at work producing him ages before he was born, that because out of these infinite combinations he was born without it? If he is, then there should be a new definition for justice. Is he to blame for what he did not have and never had? Is he to blame that his machine is imperfect? Who is to blame? I do not know. I have never in my life been interested so much in fixing blame as I have in relieving people from blame. I am not wise enough to fix it. I know that somewhere in the past there entered into him something missed. It may be defective nerves. It may be a defective heart or liver. It may be defective endocrine glands. I know it is something. I know that nothing happens in this world without a cause.'[1]

When we apportion blame we assume that the accused committed his or her crime of their own free will, while those whose actions were not under their control at the time can expect to be exonerated. Temporary insanity and coercion are respectable courtroom defences, yet, as Darrow pointed out, there is a sense in which ultimately nobody's actions are ever under their control. Actions are like any other physical events in that they all have a cause. We may trace the causal route of the murder to Loeb's intention, and that intention to his character. But his character also has a history, a set of causes that made it what it was. We can regress until we alight on causes outside the accused's control. Leopold and Loeb cannot be responsible for what occurred prior to their birth.

In the event, the pair escaped the death penalty and were sentenced to life plus ninety-nine years. Darrow's successful defence was an invocation of the philosophical theory known as 'determinism', according to which no events – not even human actions – are outside the jurisdiction of the immutable laws of nature. Just as the law of gravity causes an apple to fall to the earth, physiological laws operate upon your body and nervous system and govern your interactions with the environment and other individuals. What we think of as 'choices' are in fact the only possible outcomes in the circumstances. In short, there is no difference between what you do and what you are able to do. If determinism is true, then there is no role for free will in our behaviour and we need a new concept of responsibility.

The idea that our actions and their consequences are preordained was recognized in the ancient notion of Fate, but it was not until the Middle Ages that the doctrine of determinism was fully developed as a consequence of Christian theological beliefs. Christian philosophers reasoned that if God is omniscient, then He must know how each of us will behave in the future. But if our future actions are already known to Him, or if they could be so known in principle, then they must, in a sense, already exist, leaving us powerless to change them. This line of thinking was bolstered rather than undermined by the Scientific Revolution and the mechanical universe of Isaac Newton. The Newtonian world view seemed to show that if we could know everything about both the laws of nature and the objects upon which they operate, it would be possible in theory to predict the future destination of all things that were subject to those laws. As the French mathematician and astronomer Pierre Simon Laplace was to put it in 1820:

> Given for one instant an intelligence which could comprehend all
> the forces by which nature is animated and the respective situations
> of the beings who compose it – an intelligence sufficiently vast to

submit these data to analysis – it would embrace in the same
formula the movements of the greatest bodies of the universe and
those of the lightest atom; for it, nothing would be uncertain and
the future, as the past, would be present to its eyes.[2]

There would be such a thing as destiny after all, only it would lack
the dramatic connotations we have come to expect. Even the most
mundane life would bear the mark of fate.

One might hope to blunt determinism by locating our agency
beyond the physical world in an ethereal realm where one's soul
could make decisions unmolested by material causes and effects. In
fact, this scenario would make no difference, since the force of
determinism holds whether causes are earthly or heavenly. So long as
a cause determines one's behaviour, it makes no difference whether
the shove comes from matter or spirit. Our choices need to be caused
by *something* and determinists believe that whatever 'causes' them
must shape those choices in every detail. Something would have to
cause even a spirit's choices. Neither would the problem be solved by
the discovery of a hitherto unknown sector in the brain that was
capable of overriding the inputs of society and body chemistry. We
would only have relocated the object under discussion and would
now have to ask on what basis this substance makes choices, and by
what means it reaches its decisions. The issue is one of time rather
than space. Every choice bar an act of pure caprice has a history.
Decisions are made in the moment but conceived in the past. The
past is the source of the present, and if an earlier state of affairs causes
a later one, then it does not just prompt or precipitate it but
determines what that event is like. The problem is how to reconcile
this logic with the undeniable sensation of freedom that we all

experience, for it certainly feels as though we can choose one thing rather than another.

Other philosophers have hoped that a newer science would rescue us from the old. Events such as the decay of a radioactive particle seem to be entirely random and unpredictable. While we can say that an atom of the substance has been caused to decay, the causes do not seem to specify the particular rate of that decay down to the last alpha particle emitted. However, if random events on the quantum level were found to influence our decisions it would leave us no better off. An element of chance could not give us quite the power to originate acts that we are looking for. If I could have acted otherwise by the intercession of a random event in my brain, then this seems no different to being coerced or constrained by an event from the outside. Acts of pure caprice are not the only examples of choice, and free whim is not quite the same thing as free will. An element of chance in the decision-making process might even damage our ability to function as free agents. Most of us rather hope that our actions are efficiently determined – so long as they are determined by our nature, our preferences and our desires.

Friedrich Nietzsche, the philosopher who inspired Leopold and Loeb, would never have appeared in Chicago as a witness for the defence. He was an early exponent of a solution to the problem of free will and determinism that has attained widespread approval today. In his finest work, *On the Genealogy of Morals*, he wrote:

> To demand of strength that it should *not* express itself as strength is just as absurd as to demand of weakness that it should express itself as strength … For just as the popular mind separates the lightning from its flash and takes the latter for an *action*, for the operation of

a subject called lightning, so popular morality also separates strength from expressions of strength, as if there were a neutral substratum behind the strong man, which was *free* to express strength or not to do so. But there is no such substratum; there is no 'being' behind doing, effecting, becoming; 'the doer' is merely a fiction added to the deed – the deed is everything. The popular mind in fact doubles the deed; when it sees the lightning flash, it is the deed of a deed: it posits the same event first as cause and then a second time as its effect.[3]

This was an early expression of the view known as 'compatibilism', according to which both the determinism of the physical world and our subjective experience of freedom can be preserved.

Compatibilists believe that libertarians (in the metaphysical, not political, sense) ask too much of freedom. We begin by wanting to be free from physical coercion. Then we want to be free from undue influences on our decisions, such as people lying to us, spiking our drink with drugs or dominating us by the force of their personality. We might also want to be free from our own weaknesses, such as an addiction to alcohol or a tendency towards selfishness. But if we want to be free in an absolute sense – that is, in the sense that *nothing whatsoever* can rigidly determine our behaviour – then this would involve being free from every part of oneself, the good parts included. If we were truly free from our beliefs and opinions, our likes and dislikes, our every preference, then there would be nothing left of us *to be* free. The desire for absolute freedom terminates in a desire for the dissolution of one's selfhood, because the only thing we could mean by someone who is free in this way would be for them to be nothing at all. Since we can make no sense of a choice free from all influences, we will have to find a way of locating freedom in a world of influences that are not themselves freely chosen.

We are constantly told in newspapers and magazines, through their distillations of the latest results of the sciences, that we are 'at the mercy' of this or that drive or inclination. But one's desires are part of one's make-up, and if we take these and other personal characteristics away there is nothing left to be at the mercy of anything. It makes no sense to say that you are at the mercy of *yourself*, because what else would one expect? It would be strange indeed if this were *not* the case. If someone takes hold of your arms and forces you to act in a certain way, you feel your limbs being moved against your will. But if someone should take hold of your will itself, your very desires, and force them into a shape of their own design, what could you use to struggle against this? You have your body, your mind – and what else? Perhaps you have an immortal soul that could carry on the battle after your body and mind have fallen, but these defensive lines must stop somewhere. Once the soul was in turn overcome – however this might be accomplished – there is nowhere left for a further struggle to take place.

A prisoner who requires no walls to keep him in check is a slave. A slave who requires no whip to bend his will is a puppet, and a puppet is not an agent at all but a mere extension of its controller. We may be unfortunate enough to find ourselves prisoners, but that is a matter of others' intervention rather than our metaphysical nature. A frustrated will is a will nonetheless. The determinist, by contrast, believes that we are slaves of a sort. However, his view implies a violence that does not take place. When the determinist says that your choices are 'determined', this is a forceful word implying that your will could be contrary to the will of the world, and that the latter is somehow stronger than your own and able to overpower it.

According to compatibilist philosophers, the most celebrated being Daniel Dennett, it is simply not possible to be at odds with the world in this way. Dennett is a large man with Father Christmas whiskers and a booming voice. He was born in Beirut in 1942, where his father studied Islamic history and his mother taught English. His father worked for the forerunner of the CIA – the Office of Strategic Services – during the Second World War, and died in a plane crash while on a mission in Ethiopia in 1948. Dennett's high-achieving New England family assumed that their son would grow up to be a professor at Harvard, but he shunned the Ivy League to teach liberal arts undergraduates at the nearby Tufts University, finding beginners better at keeping him alert. As he explained to me in his modest office at Tufts: 'Younger students are not afraid to tell the Emperor that he has no clothes.' Dennett argues that, although we naturally think of action, or agency, as something that makes a difference to the world, something that 'disturbs the natural course of events', nothing of the sort actually happens since we are ourselves part of nature. It may seem to us that the asteroid 'was going to hit the Earth' until we sent all those nuclear missiles to blast it to smithereens, whereas we don't say this of all the asteroids that have been interrupted by other celestial bodies such as Jupiter or the moon during their 'collision course' with the Earth. In neither case was 'the course of nature' changed in any way. The impact simply was not determined in advance, and if anything was inevitable it was the other collision, with either moon or missile.

Incompatibilists argue that this kind of thinking is merely dressed-up determinism – in other words, that it amounts to the existence of iron fate but massages language to preserve our everyday talk of choices. In a sense, this is exactly what it is. By contrast, incompatibilists insist that real freedom requires the possibility that you could have acted otherwise. If there was only one choice you could have made, then that is no choice at all.

Suppose, one morning in the office, your boss presents you with an enticing offer: a new posting has opened up overseas and he thinks that you would make an ideal candidate for the job. He understands that you have a settled family in your current area, with three children in local schools and that your partner enjoys a wide circle of friends and works nearby in a good job of his or her own. After considering the upheaval that this will cause your loved ones and talking it over with your partner, you decide to take up the offer due to the large rise in salary it promises. However, when you tell your boss of your decision, he says that it is just as well, because he has already appointed a successor in your present role and arranged temporary accommodation for yourself and your family close to your new workplace abroad. It now seems that you had no choice at all, that the decision had already been made for you. Yet nothing has changed in one sense – you did not choose under duress since there was none that you were aware of. The physical and mental process by which you came to your decision was the same as if your boss had left the outcome open all along.

In the seventeenth century, the English philosopher John Locke wrote of how a man might 'be carried whilst fast asleep into a room where there is a person he longs to see and speak with, and be there locked fast in, beyond his power to get out; he awakes and is glad to find himself in such desirable company, which he stays willingly in'.[4] The compatibilist sees that we are constantly in this happy predicament. The natural world ensures that there is only ever one choice we can make in a given situation but, because our will is itself part of the natural world, it is invariably the one we desire. If a pessimist, or rather a determinist, calls this a 'straitjacket', he or she must remember that it is one so well tailored that it allows our every desired movement. To put it another way, a cage that moves whenever you move cannot rightly be called a cage. This may be mere wordplay, but then the compatibilist would argue that a linguistic or conceptual muddle is the root cause of deterministic worries.

When we are aware of duress from the outset, it can be very difficult to disentangle our feelings from our fears. If our office worker had discovered a memo outlining their intended fate, then their deliberations would have been very different. In moments of self-deception – the 'bad faith' of the existentialists – we are apt to tell ourselves that we actually desire to take those choices that we are not strong enough to decline. Some bloody-minded individuals are even prepared to forgo their desires for the very reason that they would have faced compulsion were their wishes different. Perhaps those possessed of flawless self-knowledge will always know when they are acting freely, but who can claim such transparency? Without such practised clarity we are forever left doubting our choices. Far from requiring the knowledge that we could have done otherwise, to be truly free is to know that you could *not* have acted differently had there been no constraints on your behaviour. Curiously, folk wisdom maintains that a man or woman's 'true' character is to be divined from those occasions when they have few options available – 'Just wait until they've got their back to the wall, then you'll find out what they're really like!' A far better sense of what someone is 'really' like can be garnered from how they act – how they *must* act – when they are at the peak of their powers and have the luxury of many paths.

Where character is concerned, ordering death from the Oval Office is more telling than cutting the throat of one's captor.

However, we can still make sense of choice even in cases where options are extremely limited. Coercion does not disqualify responsibility if someone actually wanted to commit the atrocities that they were under pain of death to carry out. For example, Nazi officers who refused to obey orders might have been shot for disobedience, but many of them did not require this threat and were quite happy to torture and kill innocents. There is a moral difference between Nazis who were only obeying orders and those whose orders happened to coincide with what they wished to do – although at the Nuremberg trials the difference may have been difficult to discern. Something may make it impossible for you to avoid a certain act without being the reason for your committing it. For example, you may be about to perform a parachute jump when the plane's engines fail. This calamity makes jumping absolutely necessary, but you were going to do it anyway. When we excuse a person who has been coerced, we do so not because they could not have acted otherwise, but because the coercion was their only reason for doing it. The question is one of motivations rather than opportunities.

Though few of us are slaves, all of us may nevertheless be puppets. What is at issue is whether we ever actually act at all, or whether things just 'happen' to us. How are we to differentiate actions from mere bodily events, a raised salute from an involuntary tic hanging over from one's army days? The obvious answer is that I *choose* to do the former, whereas the latter just *happens*. But what exactly constitutes this 'choice'? The choice cannot be my *resolution* to salute when my commanding officer marches past on the parade ground, because I could always change my mind at the last minute.

A man in England once received a prison sentence for attempted robbery even though his 'attempt' consisted of tripping over the threshold of the bank and knocking himself unconscious before he had a chance to announce his purpose. The tellers who administered first aid found an imitation firearm and a handwritten note in his pocket, which read: 'Put all the money into the bag.' This man certainly did not manage to commit a crime, but was he not so incompetent that he failed even to attempt one? He might well have lost his nerve as he approached the counter, but he was punished nonetheless. Perhaps we should allow 'choices' to be revisable prior to the final action, but we also feel that choices are full, resounding actions in themselves that, once made, are made forever.

If 'choices' are such as to truly commit one to action, then we never perceive them. In everyday life, as in Nietzschean philosophy, action is the only reliable test for intention. An experiment conducted in 1985 seems to confirm this. The American physiologist Benjamin Libet asked a group of subjects to move their fingers and to note the precise moment of their decision to do so by a stopwatch. He also placed electrodes on their scalps to detect the motor cortical activity in their brains that initiated the finger movement. He found that this activity began a third to half a second before his subjects were aware of making a conscious decision to move their fingers.[5] This in fact tallies with normal experience, in which we never catch ourselves in the act of making a final choice until we have acted and the instance has passed. We have all heard the expression: 'I don't know what I want to do. I'll wait and see what I do, and that will be what I wanted to do.' Imagine you are on a diet, yet you choose burger and fries for lunch rather than a salad. You wish that you had chosen otherwise and afterwards curse your weakness. But you regret more than just the decision – you also regret being the source of the action, in this case a source that is greedy and self-indulgent. If our decisions could not shape our character or indicate its nature, then we would not be so worried when we made lamentable choices. We despise our moral failures not because they cut against our character, but because we suspect that they reveal its true form.

To return to the metaphysical debate, in the compatibilist version of events, the human agent seems to get subsumed into the universe's general causal flow. The willing agent is not a special part of nature, walled off from the past and the future so that free choice can take place, but an ordinary (if extremely complicated) part of nature. It is for this reason that the American philosopher Thomas Nagel writes:

> I believe that in a sense the problem [of freewill and determinism] has no solution, because something in the idea of agency is incompatible with actions being events, or people being things. But as the external determinants of what someone has done are gradually exposed, in their effect on consequences, character and choice itself, it becomes gradually clear that actions are events and people things. Eventually nothing remains which can be ascribed to the responsible self, and we are left with nothing but a portion of the larger sequence of events, which can be deplored or celebrated, but not blamed or praised.[6]

Jesus advocated something similar when he exhorted us to 'hate the sin but love the sinner'. But Nagel doubts whether we will be able to achieve this, because we are unable to view ourselves simply as portions of the world. From inside, we are aware of a boundary between 'what is us and what is not, what we do and what happens to us, what is our personality and what is an accidental handicap'. As a result, he argues, 'We do not regard our actions and our characters merely as fortunate or unfortunate episodes – though they may also be that ... Those acts remain ours and we remain ourselves, despite the persuasiveness of the reasons that seem to argue us out of existence.'[7]

The concern is that if there is no source of agency distinct from the causal flow of the universe, then we cannot really talk of agents at all, which leaves human beings as mere puppets. Puppets, however, require a puppet master. The philosopher John Martin Fischer imagined just such a figure – the evil Dr Black, also known as 'the Nefarious Neurosurgeon'. While performing an operation on Jones to remove a brain tumour, Black secretly inserts a microchip into Jones's brain that enables the neurosurgeon to monitor and control his patient's behaviour via a computer. Shortly after his recovery, Jones decides to vote in the American presidential election, which is when Black's computer is programmed to swing into action. If Jones shows an inclination to decide to vote for Carter, then the computer, through the chip in Jones's brain, intervenes to make him decide to vote for Reagan. But if Jones decides to vote for Reagan of his own accord, the computer does nothing but continue to monitor Jones's behaviour.[8]

Suppose now that Jones decides to vote for Reagan on his own, just as he would have if Black had *not* inserted the mechanism into his head. Jones may think that he could have acted or, more importantly, willed otherwise, but the possibility is an illusion. The chip is a special form of prison that negates the will at its source. The difference between the machinations of the neurosurgeon and the dominion of nature is that in the former there is another individual human being in control of us. These are not fundamentally different categories of cause, but they carry very different forms of value and proffer different answers to the question of our freedom. It clearly matters whether the device – or any other cause that informs our choices – is under the control of another *individual*. Many of the problems with free will start with determination at the hands of a particular individual, and then go on to encompass gods, natural forces or 'life' itself. We should not allow our enemy to advance so far.

Imagine that Dr Black, instead of just inserting a chip, managed to alter Jones's neural pathways in a way that changed his character. The patient goes under the anaesthetic as a law-abiding citizen but wakes up as a violent criminal. He does not understand why he feels these aggressive impulses, but he is as comfortable with them as he was with his formerly placid nature. Suppose that Jones is then apprehended while carrying out an armed robbery and brought before a court of law. His defence team might well argue that it should be Dr Black facing the charges rather than their client, just as Clarence Darrow cited Richard Loeb's ancestry. Poor Jones, for his part, never intended to become a miscreant. Though there may be no option but to keep him locked up where he cannot harm the public, we will feel differently towards Jones from the way we do towards those who take up wrongdoing via more natural means. To anyone viewing him through the Perspex barrier that prevents him from attacking the jury, there is no doubt that Jones is a vicious individual, but morally speaking, we regard the explanation for how he came to be one as significant.

This is not to say that we *ought* to regard it as significant. It is merely a description of common-sense moralizing. The accused is now a bad man on any account – he has bad desires and given half a chance will act on them. However, our intuition tells us that to judge someone to be wicked is not a matter of describing their mental state alone. Being free is not a matter of feeling unfettered, or being at one with yourself, sound and single of purpose. It is a matter of history, and it seems that we attach more weight to some histories than to others. In another world, Jones might have been a psychopath all his life, made so by events in his early childhood, or in the genetic make-up of his parents prior to his conception. To exonerate Jones on the basis of Black's intervention seems to betray a prejudice in favour of recent causes over the more distant. Perhaps a benevolent neurosurgeon could 'cure' Jones and thereby make him 'free' again ('Phew, it was terrible in there! You wouldn't believe the things they made me do!'). But if Black's handiwork could not be undone, it would be odd to say that Jones could never again act freely – even fifty years hence – because of that single event in his life. The issue is the presence or absence of control.

Dennett writes:

Consider a deer in Magdalen College Park. Is it imprisoned? Yes, but not much. The enclosure is quite large. Suppose we moved the deer to a larger enclosure – the New Forest with a fence around it. Would the deer still be imprisoned? In the state of Maine, I am told, deer almost never travel more than five miles from their birthplace during their lives. If an enclosure were located outside the normal unimpeded limits of a deer's lifetime wanderings would the deer enclosed be imprisoned? Perhaps, but note that it makes a difference to our intuitions whether some*one* installs the enclosure ... Do you feel imprisoned on Planet Earth – the way Napoleon was stuck on Elba? It is one thing to be born and live

on Elba, and another to be put or kept on Elba *by someone*. A jail
without a jailer is not a jail.[9]

This is important, Dennett suggests, because our concern follows
from confusing the concepts of control and causation. 'The Viking
spacecraft,' he continues, 'is as deterministic a device as any clock, but
this does not prevent it from being able to control itself. Fancier
deterministic devices [such as ourselves] can not only control themselves; they can evade the attempts of other self-controllers to control
them.'

Moreover, Dennett adds:

The past does not control us. It no more controls us than the people
at NASA can control the spaceships that have wandered out of
reach in space. It is not that there are no causal links between the
Earth and those craft. There are; reflected sunlight from Earth still
reaches them, for instance. But causal links are not enough for
control. There must also be feedback to inform the controller.
*There are no feedback signals from the present to the past for the past
to exploit*.[10]

Few people would regard the Viking lander as free enough for our
purposes, even if it were more sophisticated. Suppose the nefarious
neurosurgeon were to die in a road accident on his way to the lab,
leaving his machinery working away in Jones's brain. He may no
longer be able to make changes in the program but his design lives
on nonetheless, albeit stuck on its final setting. It might seem to Jones
as if his nemesis has cheated death and now reaches out to control
him 'from beyond the grave'. Depending on the relative importance

of the past to our present, and the efficacy of the device in Jones's case, this is something we will have to live with. Dennett has nonetheless shown that we can drive a wedge between causation and control, and that we can talk of self-control without adding that we are always controlled in turn by something else. As Robert Nozick puts it: 'No one has ever announced that because determinism is true thermostats do not control temperature.'[11]

Dennett is a philosopher unafraid to propose – and claim – positive solutions to philosophical problems. Many of his critics dislike the way in which he uses science to settle philosophical questions, while some seem to dislike the very idea of a solution to a philosophical puzzle. As Dennett told me at the end of our meeting: 'Sometimes you get the problem articulated and the answer is clear. Free will is a good example. But there is so much backsliding. You can point out that an illusion is an illusion, and people agree. Yet then they just go on suffering for it.'

Compatibilism is a rare example of a philosophical theory that has been successful without following on from any scientific discoveries. However, it has not garnered universal acceptance. The situation is that most philosophers who work on the question of free will are incompatibilists, while most of those who do not are compatibilists. The former camp often ridicules the latter for their unfamiliarity with the latest arguments and texts on the subject. But perhaps compatibilist philosophers have better things to do than reoccupy secured ground.

The poker champion Doyle Brunson once advised card players not to ignore their extra-sensory perception during games, remarking that 'although scientists don't believe in it, how many world championship poker bracelets have scientists won?' We might also ask how non-theologians can regard the matter of Mary's virginity as settled, or how people who are not UFO fanatics can consider the alien abduction question settled. The answer, of course, is very easily. The last twenty years of the free-will debate have produced a strong line of anti-compatibilist thinking. This, however, is what one would expect in a field that has been vacated by philosophy's regular armies and left to partisans who refuse to accept defeat.

3
minds and machines

I thought of what I called an 'automatic sweetheart',
meaning a soulless body which should be absolutely
indistinguishable from a spiritually animated maiden,
laughing, talking, blushing, nursing us, and performing all
feminine offices as tactfully and sweetly as if a soul were
in her. Would anyone regard her as a full equivalent?
Certainly not.

William James

At the end of the century the use of words and general
educated opinion will have altered so much that one will
be able to speak of machines thinking without expecting
to be contradicted.

Alan Turing

Computer models of the mind no more imply that the
mind is a computer than computer models of the economy
imply that the economy is.

Hugh Mellor

Since the earliest days of philosophy, the latest technology has often
been used as a model for understanding the mind. As the American
philosopher John Searle observes:

In my childhood we were always assured that the brain was a
telephone switchboard ... Sherrington, the great British

neuroscientist, thought that the brain worked like a telegraph system. Freud often compared the brain to hydraulic and electromagnetic systems. Leibniz compared it to a mill, and I am told that some of the ancient Greeks thought the brain functions like a catapult. At present, obviously, the metaphor is the digital computer.[1]

In all the metaphors listed above, it is the mechanisms of the objects and not their materials that are important. If the Greeks ever did think that the mind worked like a catapult, this was not because they believed it to be made of wood and rope. Aristotle believed the mind to be the organizing principle of the body: 'That is why we can wholly dismiss as unnecessary the question whether the soul and the body are one: it is as though we were to ask whether the wax and its shape are one.'[2] Aristotle's teacher Plato had thought, on the contrary, that the mind was composed of a different kind of substance from the body, and philosophers from St Thomas Aquinas to René Descartes inherited his vision. However, it is Aristotle who holds the floor today, with a view of the mind as a process rather than a separate object. The modern project of artificial intelligence research contends that this process is computation.

The first cinematic depiction of artificial intelligence was in Fritz Lang's 1926 classic *Metropolis*. The film was set in a dystopian industrial society of the future and features a female android fashioned to resemble a workers' leader. As the android's face takes shape and its eyes open to reveal a perfect likeness, its proud creator remarks that 'All she lacks is a soul'. Yet this disadvantage does not prevent the android from being taken for a normal woman. The lack of a soul would not bother AI researchers today, if only they could get one of their designs to hold a proper conversation with a person. The ability to be convincing in everyday chat is the condition of the 'Turing Test', proposed by the British mathematician and inventor of the digital computer, Alan Turing, in 1950.[3] In what he called the 'imitation game', an interrogator sits in a room connected to two other rooms via a terminal. In each of the other rooms is a test subject, one a human and the other a computer. The interrogator asks the human and the computer questions through his terminal, and if he cannot tell which is the artificial mind and which the 'real' mind, then it makes sense to count them both as real. Strictly speaking, it is not the computer that would be the mind – the mind would be the software program that runs on the computer. If all minds, including those of humans, function in this way, then human consciousness is what happens when a certain kind of software is running on the hardware of the brain.

Turing himself believed that his test would be passed by the year 2000. However, the turn of the millennium has come and gone, and we are still waiting. AI researchers clearly have some explaining to do. They might try blaming Hollywood for raising our expectations. While the movies have given us armies of super-intelligent robots from C3PO to the Terminator, the technology of the real world has lagged far behind. Computer hardware may have been around for half a century now, but it has never been up to the task in hand. For most of computing history, researchers have had to contend with machinery that can barely reproduce the brainpower of an insect. Even if the hardware were up to the job, there would still be the problem of designing the right kind of software to produce human-like intelligence. The brain would have faced a similar problem during its own evolution since, physiologically, our brains are the same today as they were thousands of years ago, before we developed religion, mathematics, art and literature.

Some philosophers and scientists believe that brain architecture and linguistic culture were mutually reinforcing and that this drove the evolution of human intelligence – just as happens in the computer industry, where new software applications require faster machines to run them better, which in turn make better applications possible. This process is beginning to pay dividends. If AI enthusiasts have been over-optimistic in the past, its critics have been too pessimistic. For example, the American philosopher Hubert Dreyfus once promised that a computer would never be able to beat him at chess, only for Maurice Greenblat's 'Machack' programme to do so shortly afterwards in 1967. In his 1986 book *Mind Over Machine*, co-written with his brother Stuart, Dreyfus modestly explained that although computers could beat players at his level, it was unlikely that they would ever be able to overcome a true master. In 1997, however, IBM's 'Deep Blue' defeated the reigning world champion Gary Kasparov, regarded by chess authorities as the best human player ever to have lived. Few would say that Deep Blue 'thinks' in the fullest sense of the word. It is a very fast but ultimately mindless number-crunching machine. However, as computers become more adept at chess, face-recognition and many other tasks that were once the sole province of human minds, to disqualify their achievement may begin to look more and more like a prejudice against silicon.

The human brain possesses a hundred billion neurons which process information at an estimated rate of between a hundred million and a hundred billion MIPS (millions of instructions per second). By contrast, the first Apple Macintosh, introduced in 1984, ran at around 0.5 MIPS – comparable with a bacterium. The best desktop machines today can manage a thousand MIPS, while the fastest supercomputer weighs in at ten million MIPS. As for memory, the brain's one hundred trillion synapses are estimated to hold the equivalent of one hundred million gigabytes of information, whereas the humble 1984 Mac possessed a mere eighth of one megabyte.[4] Over the past fifty years, however, advances in computing power have observed 'Moore's Law' – proposed in 1965 by Gordon Moore, the co-founder of Intel – according to which the power of computer chips doubles every eighteen months to two years. If Moore's Law continues to hold, then on conservative estimates computers will have reached a level of performance comparable to the human brain some time before 2019.[5] In all likelihood, the main protagonists in the debate over whether a computer can have a mind will have an answer one way or another within their lifetimes.

John Searle is certain that he already has the answer, for he believes that no computer could possess a mind even if it passed the Turing Test. I met Searle in the place he describes as 'paradise' – the neo-Roman idyll of Berkeley College, California, where he has worked since 1959. Searle has a well-earned reputation as a philosophical bruiser. With a dense, compact frame, he swaggered backwards and forwards across his office with hips thrust out, emphasizing each point with a jab of his fist. He produces a stream of intricate logical reasoning to attack his bugbears, but really comes to life when loudly denouncing them as 'bullshit' at the beginning and end of each diatribe. He is exhilarating company, which is no doubt why he receives repeat invitations from such social luminaries as the Getty family. As a young assistant professor at Berkeley, Searle became involved in the Free Speech Movement, joining a student protest in 1964. His interest was only prompted because the college authorities had banned him from delivering a speech criticizing McCarthyism. For the rest of the time he found the constant protests an annoying disruption to his philosophy classes, and he dismissed the political left as evil and the right as stupid. When the students succeeded in overthrowing the Berkeley College authorities, Searle joined the new leadership for a while until they found he was resistant to socialist dogma and he tired of making enemies. However, he has never tired of making enemies within his own field. Among them are the late French thinker Jacques Derrida – in the 1970s they clashed over an abstruse interpretation of the English philosopher J.L. Austin's work – and Daniel Dennett in a feud that sprawled across the pages of the *New York Review of Books*. Readers were treated to a volley of letters in which the two philosophers progressively questioned each other's integrity, sanity, hearing and eyesight.

Searle's most famous contribution to philosophy is the Chinese Room thought experiment.[6] This has been so influential that the computer scientist Patrick Hayes once defined cognitive science as 'the ongoing research program of showing Searle's Chinese Room Argument to be false'.[7] Searle imagined a native English speaker locked in a room with a number of boxes containing Chinese characters. People outside the room can pass questions to him by posting a string of Chinese characters through the letter box. The man also possesses a very long instruction manual containing tables that enable him to cross-reference the characters and post back the correct answers by using the symbols stacked in the boxes. By this means he could conduct a conversation, albeit an extremely slow one, with a native Chinese speaker. However, it is clear that the man locked in the room does not understand Chinese. He does not know what the symbols stand for and cannot understand the questions he is asked, nor the answers he gives. His activity consists not in intelligently conversing, but in mindlessly manipulating a database of symbols according to a program of rules. Since this process is essentially what AI programs use to interact with questioners, it follows that computers do not understand English no matter how quickly and efficiently they search through their databases and produce their outputs.

One response known as the 'Systems Reply' is that the involvement of the man is a red herring. The man may not understand Chinese, but the room taken as a whole does. The man is merely the implementer of the rules, akin to a computer's Central Processing Unit (CPU). However, Searle points out that the man could memorize the contents of the boxes and the instruction manual so that the entire system is within him and he would still not have any idea what his words are about. Another approach is the 'Robot Reply', which locates the problem in the room's isolation. If a computer were fitted inside a robot body and sent out into the world with microphones and video cameras to act as 'senses', the machine would come to truly understand the language it spoke by coming into contact with the objects to which it had been unwittingly referring. Searle points out that the data received from the cameras and microphones would be fed to the CPU in the form of numerals – in other words, we would be giving the already overworked machine another set of symbols to manipulate. According to Searle, the mere *syntax* of symbols can never pull itself up by its own bootstraps and climb into the *semantics* of thought – symbols cannot interpret themselves. And it would be no good including a definition of what each symbol is supposed to denote in the programming code – as these would be couched in yet more symbols. Computers are devices that manipulate symbols according to rules. What the symbols stand for does not matter, so long as the rules are followed and each input results in the appropriate output. The interpretation of those outputs is performed by the computer's users rather than the machine itself. It is not that a machine per se cannot think – the brain is a machine, Searle attests, and brains can think – but that thinking is not a case of mindless symbol manipulation. Something needs to breathe life into the symbols to give them meaning and, to Searle, this component is the consciousness 'generated' by biological brains.

Paul and Patricia Churchland, a husband-and-wife team of philosophers, object that Searle has no right to claim that semantics cannot grow out of syntax, that meaning cannot be achieved from the bottom up, as this is an empirical matter to be settled by scientific study rather than armchair speculation. In their offices high up in the futuristic campus of the University of San Diego, they assured me that Searle's position represents a failure of imagination similar to that of the poets William Blake and Wolfgang von Goethe, who found it inconceivable that the small particles we now call 'photons' might be responsible for light. One could argue that the essential property of light is luminance, while electricity and magnetism are forces, and since forces by themselves are not constitutive of luminance, electricity and magnetism cannot be sufficient for light. One would, of course, be wrong, though the argument seemed eminently reasonable before we understood the parallels between the properties of light and those of electromagnetic waves. In 1864, the physicist James Clerk Maxwell suggested that light and electromagnetic waves were identical. This prompted the Churchlands to suggest a nineteenth-century version of Searle's experiment, which they call the 'Luminous Room':

Consider a dark room, containing a man holding a bar magnet or charged object. If the man moves the magnet vigorously up and down, then, according to Maxwell's programme of AL (artificial luminance), it will initiate a spreading circle of electromagnetic waves, and will thus be luminous. But as all of us who have toyed with magnets or charged pith balls well know, their forces or any other forces for that matter, even when set in motion, produce no luminance at all. It is inconceivable that you might constitute real luminance just by moving forces around![8]

We all know that such a room would be pitch-black inside, but this is because the frequency of the magnet's oscillations would be too low – by a factor of 10 to the power 15. The wavelength of the electromagnetic waves produced will be far too long and their energy too weak for human eyes to detect them. This, however, is a matter of quantities rather than qualities. If the frequency of the oscillations was increased sufficiently, there would come a point at which the room would be illuminated. Similarly, although *Searle's* Chinese Room might not understand Chinese, this need not mean that no room operating on the same principles could ever understand Chinese.

According to Searle, a functioning Chinese Room simulates the understanding of Chinese without understanding the essence of the language. However, it is strange to divide the essence of a skill from the ability to employ it successfully. It certainly wouldn't make sense the other way around. You could not be said to understand the essence of Chinese if you could not speak it. Perhaps if the mechanism in the room were to work much faster and were given enough contact with the world, it would inevitably gain a foothold into the meaning of its symbols. Words are able to mean what they do because they are placed in constant relationships with actions and objects. Computer syntax acquires meaning because we tie certain symbols into constant causal relationships with the world via programming and the engineering of peripherals. If an outbreak of food poisoning suddenly wiped out a road monitoring centre, the station's traffic cameras and computers would continue to represent the road network, at least until the power ran out, because the same causal relationships between the monitors and the monitored would continue to hold.

However, it is no use expecting the causal relationships of computer programs to furnish their symbols with meaning if, as Searle also alleges, they do not possess the right kind of causal powers to be conscious. Searle believes that computer simulations of the brain processes that produce consciousness stand in relation to real consciousness as a computer simulation of digestion stands in relation to real digestion. 'It's just bullshit,' he scoffed, 'because a simulated stomach can't actually digest anything. A simulated mind can't understand anything. No one expects that you could stuff a pizza into a perfect computer simulation of the digestive process.' However, other kinds of simulation seem to give us what we want. When we call up the calculator function on a desktop computer, the image of a pocket calculator appears on the screen. We don't complain that 'it isn't really a calculator', because the physical attributes of the device do not matter. Here, a simulation is as good as the real thing. What is essential are the results that each incarnation produces when you punch in the numbers, which are the same in both cases. The question, then, is whether the important 'results' of consciousness are a matter of abstraction or embodiment. You could even say it is the *entire* question, and one that cannot be settled by stipulating that the results must be conceived in biological brains. For artists, acrylic paint simulates the effect of oil colours. A retinal scanner simulates the effect of a key. What matters is that the door opens, not that the tool is made of carved nickel alloy. If a pocket calculator does *real* calculation because the results of its operations – numbers on a screen – have an equivalence with or are interchangeable with the numbers written on a mathematician's blackboard, the question is whether the products of consciousness – words and expressions – are more like these numbers than slices of pizza.

Searle believes that there is something special about brain tissue that enables it to generate consciousness. It is the biological function of the brain to produce thoughts just as it is the function of the heart to pump blood or the lungs to breathe air. However, this seems to talk of consciousness as a kind of 'brain glow', a discrete physical effect, and it is far from clear that it can be such a thing. Searle is a materialist, and agrees that the brain is a machine – that consciousness is the result of a machine process. It's just that a computer, he believes, is not the appropriate kind of machine with which to draw an analogy. Minds, he argues, are part of nature, but computers exist only because people regard certain objects as computers. 'Nothing is a computer in itself,' he said. 'Something only becomes a computer when it is used to compute something by a conscious agent.' He insisted that a computational interpretation could be put on anything: 'Any mundane object such as a window can be a computer – representing a one if open and a zero if closed.' Searle was returning to the point that semantics – meaning, or 'aboutness' – cannot be derived from the bottom up. And, because non-trivial computation is a higher order function of an object, there are no natural computers – nothing is, in itself, a computer before it is used as one, nor can it be its own user. Daniel Dennett's response is that brains will in fact have to be their own users, because no one else is going to do it for them. Brains succeed because they are the products of natural selection. Evolution has shaped the human brain so that its neuronal patterns react to inputs from our environment and cause a rational response to them. Likewise, the symbols manipulated inside a computer acquire their significance, their ability to do a job, by the constant relations they have with other objects outside the machine. In the case of today's computers, these objects include printers, scanners and missile tracking systems. In the future the objects may include other language users. Dennett parodies Searle's position as claiming in effect, that 'Airplane wings are really for flying, but eagles' wings are not.'[9] In a sense this is true, since no one specifically designed eagles' wings to enable them to fly. However, this does not allow us to deny that eagles fly, or that we can make sense of what they do as flying.

Philosophers who believe full AI to be possible concede that pocket calculators lack consciousness. Such 'one-track' minds are not minds at all. The mind exists, they think, when thousands of similar activities are all taking place in the computer. However, the notion of bolting on more competencies soon runs into a problem. An ordinary computer works with a serial processor – a bottleneck through which all its operations are squeezed. So at any one time it is performing a single operation, a single activity. If minds are possible in these circumstances then they are even stranger than we thought. It implies that a mind can be considered to have an existence when viewed over an expanse of time, even though it does not exist in any single moment taken by itself. One can also ask about the upper limit to this timescale. On computationalist principles alone, there is no reason why a computer should not take, say, ten billion years to complete the operations equivalent to a human adult remarking on the weather. To insist on more prompt answers would seem arbitrary. The strangeness of this thought leads one to consider an alternative form of computation.

This is the answer favoured by Searle's colleague at Berkeley – the chess-playing critic of AI, Hubert Dreyfus. Professor Dreyfus is famous in the philosophical world for disseminating the thought of the German existentialist philosopher Martin Heidegger. He is also known, and envied, for making a fortune working as a philosophical consultant to Fernando Flores, the economic whizz-kid who President Salvador Allende of Chile made finance minister at the age of twenty-nine, in his country's short-lived socialist government. Following three years in prison under General Augusto Pinochet, Flores studied under Dreyfus before starting a successful software company. With his ascetic demeanour, pale clothes and lean build, Dreyfus does not look as though he was performing this role for the money, but he does allow himself the luxury of zipping around campus in a vintage Volkswagen Karmann Ghia. Of all the philosophers I talked to during the research for this book, Dreyfus was the only one who seemed to be thinking about each question anew even when it concerned issues he had long ago left behind. One of these was artificial intelligence. 'I don't think about computers any more,' he told me. 'I figure I won and it's over – they've given up.'

Dreyfus's 'winning' argument is that human minds and computers work in very different ways. For example, a human chess player does not decide on the best move by running through thousands of positions and examining the consequences of every possible action. Instead, it might take a grand master only a few seconds to decide what to do using intuition. The grand master is using a highly developed form of common sense to rule out certain moves at the outset. He knows intuitively that certain approaches will be suicidal and does not bother to process them at all. The computer by contrast – even Deep Blue, the conqueror of Gary Kasparov – knows nothing of the sort and laboriously grinds out the consequences of moves that are 'obviously' stupid to a human player. There needs to be a way of determining what is relevant to apply the rules to, but a computer is incapable of this kind of discrimination. Common sense requires the ability to make generalizations, and such judgements are made by looking at a situation holistically rather than by applying a set of rules to one piece of information at a time. It is the difference between knowledge and 'know-how'. 'Computers, you see,' explained Dreyfus, 'possess only representations and rules for manipulating those representations, and these things simply are not involved in know-how.' It should be noted that computers' lack of common sense was one of the reasons why critics originally doubted that they would ever be able to play chess at grand-master level. But at least chess is a limited, self-contained domain with a finite number of possible moves to consider. If a computer had to face life in the everyday world, there would be too many options to process every single one.

Dreyfus agrees that, in one sense, the brain is a computer, 'in that it's a piece of meat that comes up with answers, but more interesting is whether it follows rules, whether the brain's processing is holistic or atomistic'. By this, Dreyfus means whether the brain works atom-istically like a digital computer processing strings of code according to rules, or holistically like an analogue device that learns to recog-nize patterns. The latter model is known variously as 'Parallel Distributed Processing' (PDP) and 'connectionism'. Unlike a PC, the brain does not have a CPU where every calculation is made. The brain processes information on the basis of millions of smaller units working in parallel. Each processing unit, or neuron, is arranged in a network of weighted connections that maps various pieces of information. This mapping can be fine-tuned by adjusting the weighting of the connections between neurons until the appropriate outputs are achieved. The chips inside digital computers work much faster than neurons, but because many interconnected neurons tackle the same problem simultaneously, the brain can achieve a greater speed in certain tasks. Such a 'parallel' processing architecture is more efficient at dealing with extremely multifarious inputs, such as recognizing the outline of a lion on the horizon. It is also faster at recalling how to avoid the beast, since this information is distributed across the system in the relative strengths of the connections between millions of neurons. Given the quantity of information that a brain has to store, laboriously forcing the entire catalogue through the bottleneck of a CPU to retrieve the relevant data would mean that the lion would be upon us before we remembered that we were supposed to climb a tree. For other tasks that require many transformations of a limited set of inputs – for example, a long multiplication sum – serial processors such as a desktop PC perform better than brains. The brain can, of course, perform these functions too, but they are only one of its many talents rather than its general mode of operation.

The superior virtues of parallel processing architectures do not matter to the philosophical question in hand. The former may be better if you want to avoid hungry lions, but here we are only interested in the ability to think at all, not the ability to think about certain sorts of things quickly and efficiently. It may be possible to separate thinking per se from thinking in the way that humans do, and digital computers might be able to think without the human mind serving as the example. Dennett, however, counsels us not to be too impressed by the differences, for 'at the heart of the most volatile pattern-recognition system (whether connectionist or not) lies a [serial] engine, chugging along, computing a computable function'.[10] Each individual neuron amounts to a tiny, number-crunching robot. Dennett points out further that a parallel processor can be simulated on a serial machine by calculating one connection at a time and agglomerating the results. The same tasks can be performed in this way, albeit much more slowly and one at a time. This leads to a quandary when we consider our own minds, for although we think with the speed that parallel processing allows, our thoughts are not a cacophony of competing voices. Dennett dubs the human mind a 'Joycean machine', as he believes that its parallel circuits produce a 'virtual', serial processor better known as the stream of consciousness.

The philosopher Jerry Fodor refers to the computational, or 'number-crunching', theory of mind as 'the only game in town'. When I spoke to him in New York, he told me that:

Right now, we are sure that computation is the model for the mind. But 500 years from now, when real progress has been made, it's wildly unlikely that our descendants' favoured theory is going to look anything like anything that we can imagine today. The best approximation we've got now is the computational system, but what I take for granted is that if God told you the way the mind worked, you wouldn't understand it. You wouldn't be able to *read* the last chapter. This is why I don't think it's particularly important to have a popular view.

According to the futurist Nick Bostrom, Fodor is wrong that future minds will shy away from the computer model, because they are likely to be computers themselves. But this is also why Fodor is right that we would be unable to fully understand the final chapter on the mind – because it will be written by artificial minds with intellectual faculties far greater than our own. This would have severe consequences for human self-esteem, or at least the self-esteem of philosophers of mind. From Fritz Lang's *Metropolis* to *The Matrix* of the Wachowski brothers, the movie industry has shown humans enslaved by their robotic creations. The real fear should be that such machines would render some of us superfluous. Certain philosophers are less worried by this prospect than others. John Searle writes:

> Like all games, chess is built around the human brain and body and its various capacities and limitations. The fact that Deep Blue can go through a series of electrical processes that we can interpret as 'beating the world champion at chess' is no more significant for human chess playing than it would be significant for human football playing if we built a steel robot which could carry the ball in a way that made it impossible for the robot to be tackled by human beings. The Deep Blue chess player is as irrelevant to human concerns as is the Deep Blue running back.[11]

Searle does not seem the type to worry about anything unduly, but his vision is hopeful to say the least. If the steel robots were intelligent individuals that passed the Turing Test and formed their own professional league, then human American football might stand in relation to it as the amateur game stands to the NFL today. And if artificial intelligences rather than human beings were making the scientific advances, writing the best novels and designing ever more advanced versions of themselves, then we would become as children or pets, left to amuse ourselves while superior beings did the important work.

It might be best for philosophers to stop arguing about the issue of artificial intelligence and simply wait for science to succeed or fail in producing machines that can hold a conversation. In the current literature, philosophy has two chief roles: first, to determine whether or not such machines would be conscious, and, second, to predict whether or not such machines are possible. The answer to the second is to wait and see, and then the answer to the first will be irrelevant. If talking machines are ever invented, it is likely that there will be no more argument about whether they are merely simulating conversation than there is today about whether pocket calculators merely simulate calculation. Calculators 'do the job', and a talking machine would 'do the job' of talking. There may not be a person attached to the mouthpiece, but all this means is to say that talking is the only thing the machine does, in which case, to achieve parity between man and machine we need only make sure the latter can do all our other jobs. One could object that the computer simulates lots of different small tasks, like chess playing, arithmetic solving and – hopefully, one day – novel-writing and joke-telling, but nowhere does it actually simulate a mind as opposed to one of the mind's functions. However, we could ask whether there is anything to a mind once its functions are taken away, any more than there is something to a chair once its seat, legs and backrest are taken away. This question is the subject of the next chapter.

bodies and souls

That anything so remarkable as a state of consciousness
comes about as a result of irritating nervous tissue is just
as unaccountable as the appearance of the djinn when
Aladdin rubbed his lamp.

Thomas Huxley

Science cannot give us the taste of chicken soup. But,
when you think about it, wouldn't it be weird if it did?

Albert Einstein

In 2001, a team at the University of Victoria in Canada was reported
to be developing a 'mind-reading' device for use by the severely disabled. Their 'Cyberlink' headband is designed to detect brain signals
from people who are unable to speak. Linked to a voice synthesizer,
the hope is that this information can be translated into electronic
speech. Quadriplegics such as Professor Stephen Hawking would be
spared the laborious task of communicating their thoughts one letter
at a time through a computer interface. Should a working model of
the Cyberlink be produced, it would change the way we think about
the mind–body problem. Part of the reason we find it difficult to see
how consciousness emerges from matter is that the mind and our
environment seem to occupy two entirely different worlds – one
internal, and the other external. What takes place in the external
world is a matter of public record, but the thoughts that go on in the
internal world are, we think, private and screened off from the gaze

of other individuals. If the Cyberlink ever goes on sale, this privacy will have proved to be contingent rather than representing any kind of metaphysical barrier between two worlds. Hearing our thoughts broadcast over a loudspeaker as we think them might even lead us to stop speaking of two worlds at all. But perhaps we would cite a deeper, silent level of thought that the loudspeaker fails to expose. We might suspect that what we heard was not the subject's real thoughts, but only what he or she wanted us to hear. We would be unable to prove that the subject was not deceiving us. But if everyone who was wired up to the machine reported that it worked perfectly for them, and if we also tried it out ourselves and found their testimony to be supported by our own experience, the correlation would no doubt be good enough to convince us. Such a device may prove impossible to construct, but there is no reason to think so – after all, our lips and vocal chords have no trouble translating brain signals into speech.

None of this would be possible if thoughts were not dependent upon events in the brain and nervous system. One would imagine the Cyberlink to be the world's first machine for detecting consciousness – an engineer's solution to the philosophical problem of how to prove the existence of other people's minds. It would show the problem to be the thickness of the skull and not the opacity of the mind. You can't hear my thoughts or feel my pain, but neither can you see the floater on my eyeball or feel the pretzel stuck in my throat, and no one would say that these two objects are uniquely accessible from the first-person perspective. However, some philosophers would be unimpressed, because they deny that thoughts consist in certain brain processes alone. The fear (or hope, according to one's fancy) is that even were we to discover exactly what

materials, configurations and processes are required for consciousness, we would still not have answered what the Australian
philosopher David Chalmers calls the 'Hard Problem': that is, why
any of this should result in conscious experiences. The other problems
are 'easy' by comparison because we know how to go about solving
them – it is a matter of doing more neuroscience.

Not only are we unable to say exactly how the brain produces consciousness, but we cannot explain why complicated arrangements of
neurons should produce experiences at all. The brain probably does
not have a choice in the matter, but our imagination tells us that God
would have had. In the seventeenth century, the French philosopher
René Descartes argued that he could imagine himself lacking a body
and existing as a disembodied mind. This must be possible, he held,
because mind and body possessed two distinct essences – thought
and extension respectively. Thus they must consist of different substances that, though they are always found together in this world,
could be separated if the Almighty chose. This argument for the
theory known as 'dualism' rests on the supposed indiscernibility of
identical entities, a version of 'Leibniz's Law' that states that no 'two'
objects can in fact be one and the same if there is any property that
they do not both possess. Descartes was in no doubt as to which of
these two substances he more closely identified with: 'seeing that I
could pretend that I had no body ... but that I could not, for all that,
pretend that I did not exist.... I thereby concluded that I was a substance, of which the whole essence or nature consists in thinking, and
which, in order to exist, needs no place and depends on no material
thing.'[1] Unfortunately for Descartes, Leibniz's Law has exceptions,
such as the Masked Man fallacy: I may know who my father is, but
not know the identity of a man I meet at a masked ball. This disparity

does not allow me to conclude that the masked man is not my father. If the man behind the disguise is indeed my father, then it is irrelevant that I may imagine him being someone else. The way we think about an object cannot be regarded as one of its properties in quite the same way as its inherent attributes.

It is common for contemporary philosophers of mind to begin their accounts with a rejection of Descartes, the successor to the rehabilitated Aristotle as the Typhoid Mary of philosophy. David Chalmers, however, believes that Descartes was on to something, but that he approached the problem from the wrong direction. The philosophy of mind is, for most students, a process of overturning their dualist intuitions in favour of one or other form of materialism. Only the most religious survive with their fondest beliefs, if not always with the respect of their peers, intact. Chalmers, by contrast, was a mathematician and physicist by training, who started with a sentimental attachment to materialism yet went on to become the recognized leader of the 'New Dualist' school.

Chalmers lives and works in the desert on the fringes of Tucson, Arizona. He suggested we conduct our interview outside, and sat hatless and unblinking during a two-hour conversation. While I cowered behind sunglasses, a cap and a thick layer of Factor 20, his only protection from the midday desert sun was the poodle hairstyle of a heavy-metal guitarist. 'The crucial thing isn't the conceivability of mind without body,' he told me, 'but the conceivability of body without mind – that all this physical activity could be going on without the mental activity.' In other words, where Descartes looked for ghosts, we should instead search for zombies. The kind of zombies that worry philosophers are not the green, flesh-eating variety portrayed in horror movies, but creatures that are outwardly just like you and me. They seem healthy and normal, hold down jobs and marriages and conduct cheerful conversations, but unbeknownst to us they are in fact automata. They have no internal lives – no hopes or fears or sensations – even though they may often talk as if they had them. They could even don a Cyberlink headband and the device would produce speech just as if it was worn by a conscious individual. They have all the physical attributes and behaviour of conscious beings, but without the mental qualities. One can certainly imagine a being that possesses brain processes without having an internal life to go with them.

Christof Koch and Francis Crick, who, with James Watson, discovered the structure of DNA, point out that much of human behaviour is already conducted in a zombie-like state.[2] 'Automatic' activities such as driving or rock-climbing do not usually involve thought even though they did when we were learning them. There is neuronal activity that results in intelligent behaviour that does not involve conscious deliberation. Indeed, there are certain feats, such as playing the piano to virtuoso level, that can usually only be carried out so long as we do *not* consciously deliberate. This leads to the worry that if we became sufficiently versed in every aspect of our undertakings, our every word and deed would be carried out on autopilot. Consciousness, it would seem, is only there for those things in life that we are not very good at. But one expects that the brain processes involved in conscious and non-conscious/automatic driving or rock-climbing will be slightly different. The philosophical question is whether they *must* be different, for a true zombie is mindless no matter what his brain processes are like. The answer depends on how seriously we should take our imaginative powers in this instance.

For the philosopher Daniel Dennett, the answer is not very seriously at all. Dennett came to philosophy by reading Descartes as a teenager and, believing the philosopher's dualism to be mistaken, took it upon himself to show why. Along the way he also discovered talents as a sculptor and jazz pianist that could have given him a career in either field. He is used to success and was for many years driven to distraction by philosophers who refused to see what he regards as sense. Today he seems to accept that he will never change their minds. Perhaps he lost his patience one too many times, as he seems to pity his opponents – and also himself for having expended so much breath in the cause. He chose not to mention these names when I met him. Containing himself, he told me that: 'It's very easy for very bright but appropriately insecure thinkers to get seduced into a little set of issues and just be unable or unwilling to step back from this and ask whether, in the larger scheme of things, it is worth doing. I call this "Hebb's Rule" after the great Canadian psychologist Donald Hebb. He said, "If it's not worth doing it's not worth doing well," and by golly if you live by Hebb's Rule an awful lot of philosophy wouldn't get done.'

Dennett sees no mystery in consciousness – just an engineering problem that he hopes will be solved through the application of cognitive science. To his mind:

The hard problem is one of the fascinating bits of sociology in the field. It's a straightforward fallacy of subtraction. People just aren't doing their sums correctly. They convince themselves and other people that there's this extra problem when there just isn't one. I tell a story about the 'tuned deck'. Ralph Hull was a well-regarded card magician early in the twentieth century in America who had a trick he did for his fellow magicians, an insiders' trick. He had people pick a card, listened to the 'vibrations' of the deck and then produced the card. He would change the way he did the trick each time to frustrate their guesses as to how he did it. The real trick is in the word 'The'. They were looking too hard. He made them think there was just one trick, just one theory, and got them to look for it – he fooled them into thinking there was a 'hard' problem. Now if you think that consciousness is just a bag of tricks as I have been arguing for years and years – then you don't explain all the tricks with one big explanation. You have to explain the parts independently, because they're not all the same. And if you insist that over and above all of that there's also the 'hard' problem, you have to show that there really is such a problem and that the sum of all the smaller problems does not exhaust the issue. So far, the attempts to show the existence of a hard problem have been ludicrous. Yet people just roll over and say, 'Oh, I'm not even *trying* to tackle the *hard* problem.'

Dennett likes to compare the problem of consciousness to the nineteenth-century debate between the vitalists, who believed in a life force that animated living creatures and separated them from the dead and inorganic, and mechanists, who thought the answer lay in complex natural processes.

Imagine the vitalist saying 'Yes, you've solved the "easy" problems of life – the problems of reproduction, repair and growth, metabolism and variety, but you haven't touched on the "hard" problem, which is: what is life itself?' Well, if you're a vitalist you still think there's a hard problem of life, but there isn't. When I raise this parallel it has two effects: firstly, it causes some believers in the hard problem some consternation. The other effect is to tease out of the closet latter-day vitalists who really want to believe that there is a mystery to life beyond all this darned molecular biology and DNA. They want to be vitalists still. At least I've teased them out of the closet.

David Chalmers refuses to accept the comparison with vitalism, saying:

I think there are some pretty serious differences. There are these easy problems about consciousness: explaining all the functional bits associated with the things people say and do. After you've explained all those problems there's a residual problem: why is all this accompanied by consciousness? In the other, smaller areas, it looks like when you explained the functions you explained everything about them. In the case of the problem of life, explaining the functions, explaining the behaviours were always the central problems. But back then, around 200 years ago, people couldn't see even how to solve the easy problems. How is it that a system of matter could reproduce, adapt and locomote? The mechanists thought that somehow it could; the vitalists thought that it couldn't. That was a straightforward empirical question. Even the vitalists thought that it was possible in principle – they could imagine it working that way – they just didn't think that was the way that it worked. When people did the empirical science it turned out that biological systems of the right kind could perform the functions of reproduction, locomotion and the rest. The problem went away and the vitalists just disappeared. What that suggests is that even for the vitalists, the problem was one of explaining structure and objective function all along. The easier problems of life were the only problems. What happens in the case of consciousness is that there are two different kinds of problem: there's the problem of explaining the functions, and the problem of explaining why this is accompanied by consciousness.

I suggested that water and H_2O might be a more appropriate analogy than life and matter. We might think that we can imagine water having a different molecular make-up to H_2O, but chemical physicists tell us that no other configuration would work in quite the same way to deliver all the precise properties of ordinary water. Even 'heavy' water (D_2O), in which the two oxygen atoms are replaced by deuterium, does not share all the macroscopic properties of ordinary water (it is around 10 per cent heavier than H_2O). Professor Chalmers thought this was no better:

In every other domain besides consciousness we get some kind of reductive explanation, and we have this wonderful chain of explanation from physics to chemistry to biology to psychology, eventually to economics, and so on. One level seems to be in principle capable of explaining what is at the next level without residue. You find that with H_2O and water. But there are the physical and the perceived aspects of liquidity, the same with heat and light. The physics doesn't exactly explain these because those are ultimately properties of consciousness, and we cannot explain why consciousness is the way it is. The fluid mechanics of water can be given a full explanation with a micro-chemical story, but we still can't explain why heat or wetness *feel* the way they do.

The view that elements of mind must be beyond the reach of science, as if consciousness requires a new physics, has a brief but notorious history. Frank Jackson – another Australian philosopher – imagined the story of 'Mary the neuroscientist'.[3] Mary is an expert on colour perception. She knows everything the sciences could ever tell us about what goes on inside someone's brain and nervous system when they experience colours. However, Mary conducts her research from a lifelong prison cell – a black-and-white room, with a black-and-white television, and a computer with a monochrome monitor. She has never once seen a coloured object. According to the story, no matter how much she understands of the physics and neurochemistry of colour, there is something she does not understand about redness until she steps out of the room and sees a rose with her own eyes for the first time. There is thus something about conscious perceptual experience that cannot be captured in the third-person language of the sciences. Philosophers call these entities 'qualia'. Dennett himself describes qualia as 'the souls of experiences' – and dismisses them as he does the supposed souls of human beings. He deems Mary the colour scientist:

A classic provoker of Philosophers' Syndrome: mistaking a failure of imagination for an insight into necessity. What happens is that the thought experiment begs the question. For if Mary could already understand *everything* about colour, *and if* materialism-reductionism is true and higher order properties can be read off from lower level ones – then she will indeed know about the subjective experiences attaching to redness. Asserting that she will in fact be surprised is asserting nothing more nor less than that materialism-reductionism is not in fact true, that higher-level properties cannot be so read off.

Chalmers argues that consciousness is a special case, an exception to the reductionism that has been so successful in the sciences, and his intuition demands respect due to his extensive knowledge of materialist neuroscience. The enthusiasm of some 'new dualists' is less because they are unconvinced by recent progress in the cognitive sciences than because they simply do not like that progress. This could not be said of their standard bearer, Chalmers, who agrees that we already know how some facets of thinking work and what brain states they correlate with, yet maintains that even in these limited areas of progress we have no idea why they should be so correlated. Dennett does not find this surprising:

Our uneasy relationship with scientific advances goes back to Copernicus – it still seems that the sun moves, after all. We've learned, however, not to credit that seeming. But there's a sense in which we don't have our heart in this, even though it's so exposed. There are other hunches that are like that. One is the 'zombic hunch': that when you've exposed consciousness from the third-person point of view there's this left-over problem – the problem of zombies. When you look at the definitions people have offered they're ridiculous. The idea that zombies are possible is a ludicrously bad idea, but people can't get rid of it. They can't jettison the idea even though they know that there aren't any good arguments for it. I can feel the zombie hunch as well as anyone, I've just learned not to credit that urge and regard it as something to be resisted with a grin whenever you feel the urge to assert it. David admits that he has no arguments for his decision that zombies are possible, that it's just a brute difference between the two of us. I say to him that if you admit that arguments don't play a role here, then can I suggest therapy? If he has a problem that reason won't touch, then maybe a pill or exercises will help. You try argument, you try humour, you try scaring them or joking them out of it, then you just say, well, my heart goes out to you. What else can you do?

Putting on a silly voice, Dennett added: 'We should be more ready to entertain the notion that some of our *deepest convictions* are just these things that get stuck in our heads and can't be easily dislodged. You certainly aren't going to base a science on the fact that you have this kink in your head.'

In fact, something along these lines is exactly what Chalmers would like, for he believes that the solution of the problem of consciousness requires a new leap of thought. As he said:

My own view is that you have to understand consciousness as something irreducible in the same way that a physicist takes space as irreducible – that is, you still understand space, but you don't explain it in terms of anything more basic than itself. No one would say 'We don't understand space, we don't understand time.' We take them as irreducible, but we still have theories of them. The way the science of consciousness has to proceed is more or less the same way: to admit it as an irreducible entity and then start building theories of it.

I suggested in objection that space is a building block – in that you do not need to have anything beforehand in order to have it, whereas

consciousness can hardly be a building block if it requires complicated brains and nervous systems.

Chalmers replied that it was far from clear that such apparatus is
essential. He assured me:

We don't know where consciousness is. There's this famous
problem of other minds – I can't look inside your mind and see
whether you are conscious. I can't look inside a dog's mind and see
whether it's conscious. I can't look inside a *fly's* mind and see
whether it's conscious. I do surveys of my students from time to
time – most of them are pretty confident that dogs are conscious.
With mice it's still the majority, and with flies it's around 50:50. Its
not out of the question that consciousness runs pretty deep in the
natural order. I'm agnostic on this, but I don't rule out the fact that
consciousness is grounded in a pretty fundamental level of physical
reality in the way that space is. There could be some kind of
common building block, so to speak, in physics and consciousness.
One idea which Bertrand Russell was fond of is that the intrinsic
nature of physics itself is not revealed to us – it's only revealed to us
from the outside as a network of relations: for example, one particle
causes this other particle, mass is a thing that resists acceleration in
various ways, and so on. However, the *intrinsic* nature of the
physical world is up for grabs. Russell was attracted to the idea that
this intrinsic nature might itself have something very deep to do
with consciousness. I mean, what's the fundamental, intrinsic
nature of an electron or proton? Maybe there's consciousness right
down to that level. We know from physics that electrons can be in
one position or another, or can have one kind of mass or another
but, on this hypothesis, they have very specific intrinsic natures

which are not revealed to us from the way they appear from the outside. Everything has an inside and an outside, an intrinsic and extrinsic nature. On this hypothesis, the intrinsic nature has something to do with consciousness. Things have to have some kind of intrinsic nature, and maybe it's something like *this*. And then in the right kind of configuration, it gives rise to consciousness. Russell's idea was that maybe something about the intrinsic properties of particles inside our own brains in this kind of configuration is what gives you consciousness. It's not a theory, it's just a template or framework for a theory, of thinking about consciousness or proto-consciousness as irreducible there at the bottom level of the natural order, and then the question is, how do you get from there to the kind of familiar features of consciousness that we know and love?

This was sounding like the view known as 'panpsychism', according to which mind is a fundamental feature of the universe. To the panpsychist, every tree, every pebble, every speck of dust has a mental aspect, an internal life, however simple and uneventful. Chalmers prefers to describe his position as 'panprotopsychism'. The difference between the two, he says, is that:

Under panpsychism, everything is conscious down to the subatomic level – there is something that it feels like to be an electron or a proton. I don't want to say that's completely crazy, though it's certainly weird and counter-intuitive. But the other possibility is a property that while not intrinsically consciousness, collectively constitutes consciousness in the right kind of system. It might stand to consciousness as proto-life stands to life or as basic physical processes stand to life. The question is what that would be like, and the answer is that no one has any idea. One way to think about it is that you have complex consciousness of colour, and then you can bring it down to hue and saturation, which aren't directly experienced but are components of an experience. You can break down experiences further and further into basic components until you get to a level that is under the surface of consciousness – not directly experienced in our consciousness except as a large collection. It may be possible for these things to be considered individually at the bottom of the natural order in a way in which we would not say they correspond to anything in consciousness. They would correspond instead to something like proto-consciousness.

Chalmers finds panpsychism so attractive because it bridges the perceived conceptual gap between the character of brain processes and that of the conscious experiences with which they are supposed to correlate. It changes the problem from one of explaining how consciousness arises from non-conscious constituents to that of how one form of consciousness arises from another. Chalmers also describes it as a 'strangely beautiful' picture of the world. Unfortunately, it is also a picture so far removed from what we understand of physics and biology that it is almost pure fantasy. That panpsychism has become the last redoubt of the dualist shows that this hounded species has been forced to occupy the most hostile, unforgiving niches of today's intellectual environment. At least we now know what the options are regarding consciousness: either it is derivable from lower-order quantities, or it goes 'all the way down' and is a basic property of matter.

Any difficulty in reconciling mind and matter should not push us towards the panpsychist solution, for the experience of puzzlement is not limited to our encounters with brains. Some of us feel puzzled when we look inside a hi-fi or under the hood of a car. I cannot understand how these objects work because I do not know enough about their technology. But if I completed a diploma in mechanics or sound engineering I hope that I would know very well how a car runs or a hi-fi produces music. Given current science's limited understanding of the brain, it can be difficult to see how a lump of organic tissue can give rise to the wonder of conscious experience. Brains are quiet objects unadorned with flashing lights or crackles of blue electricity running across their surfaces. However, it cannot be too difficult, as the materialist view of the mind has been accepted so widely that the debate between dualism and materialism is conducted only on the fringes of philosophy today. It may not seem this way when viewing the media, because they need to present two sides to every story in order to have a debate at all. When we listen to a radio programme in which 50 per cent of the airtime is given to someone who defends terrorism, we don't know how difficult it was for the programme's researchers to find this spokesperson. Mainstream opinion on mind and matter is better represented by the reviewers of Francis Crick's book on how the brain creates the mind. Critics took issue with the great biologist's choice of title. The problem with *The Astonishing Hypothesis*, they argued, was that there was nothing astonishing about it.

part two

what do I know?

the problem of knowledge

With me, the horrid doubt always arises whether the convictions of man's mind, which has been developed from the mind of the lower animals, are of any value or at all trustworthy. Would anyone trust in the convictions of a monkey's mind, if there are any convictions in such a mind?

Charles Darwin

Knowing one's thoughts no more requires separate investigation of the conditions that make the judgement possible than knowing what one perceives.

Tyler Burge

As we know, there are known knowns. There are things we know we know. We also know there are known unknowns. That is to say, we know there are some things we do not know. But there are also unknown unknowns, the ones we don't know we don't know.

Donald Rumsfeld

The Hollywood movie *The Matrix* imagines a future in which humans have been enslaved by machines. From birth to death, they sleep imprisoned in pods where they are fed through tubes and washed by robots. While they slumber, they believe that they have normal jobs and families, but in fact their lives are conducted in a computer-generated simulation of late twentieth-century America. For reasons known only to the machines, it is best that all humans occupy this closest sustainable approximation of Utopia – the benighted citizens of the virtual Third World presumably being high-tech cardboard cut-outs. The simulation is so detailed and faithful that no one suspects that they do not live in the physical world. Everyone has virtual hobbies and virtual relationships and, as one character remarks, steak tastes just as good in 'the Matrix' as the real thing (not that he has ever tasted the real thing). Such a paranoid fantasy may yet be the fate of humanity. There is a theory that the reason SETI (Search for Extra-terrestrial Intelligence) has so far failed to detect any signals from alien civilizations is not that sufficiently advanced cultures sooner or later destroy themselves in war, but that they decide to spend their time in a virtual reality paradise as soon as they discover how to devise one. By plugging themselves into a virtual reality of their own design, they are able to leave behind the inevitable frustrations of life in the natural world and exist free from pain and death. The period when they would be broadcasting signals would last from their invention of radio to the development of technology that can render virtual experiences at least as good as the real thing – let's say, 150 years. The thought that life in the Matrix might not be so bad after all is a comforting one because, according to one thinker, we may be in it already.

The Swedish philosopher Nick Bostrom puts the chance at around one in five.[1] He sees three possibilities for the future of humanity: either we will become extinct before the 'post-human' era in which we are able to create the Matrix, or we will decline to create a significant number of simulated people when we get there, or we are already living in the Matrix. The latter depends on the prospect of computing power continuing to increase until true artificial intelligence has been created, which Bostrom rates as very likely. This may be disputed at the outset, but the philosopher is used to making predictions, having worked as an adviser to the European Union on scientific research and the CIA on long-term security risks. Born in 1973, Bostrom is very young to be a respected philosopher. As a fifteen-year-old he wandered into his local library when bored one day and picked out a book at random: *Thus Spake Zarathustra* by Friedrich Nietzsche. Reading Nietzsche transformed his attitude to school, and in his undergraduate days he studied three full-time programmes simultaneously. He now spends his time philosophizing about a 'trans-human' future in which machine intelligence has far outstripped that of its creators and in which humans have merged with their technology and uploaded their consciousness into digital computers. These interests have garnered him more appearances in the mainstream media over the past few years than any other living philosopher bar Peter Singer and Noam Chomsky.

Bostrom maintains that once we can simulate consciousness, we may then decide to simulate worlds for artificial minds to inhabit, and might even place them within re-creations of human history without them knowing. In such a future, most minds might belong not to flesh-and-blood creatures like ourselves, but to digital individuals living inside artificial worlds. The task of constructing the artificial world could be made easier by furnishing it only with those parts that its inhabitants need to know about. For example, the microscopic structure of the Earth's interior could be left blank, at least until someone decides to dig down deep enough, in which case the details could be hastily filled in as required. If the most distant stars are hazy, no one is ever going to get close enough to them to notice that something is amiss. Other philosophers have even suggested that quantum indeterminacy is a feature of the limited resolution of our simulated world. And how are we to discern whether our own world is real or simulated? It is a simple matter of probability. If one day every PC user had such a simulation running on their computer, the ratio of simulants to 'real' people could be a billion to one. Bostrom tells us:

> If betting odds provide some guidance to rational belief, it may also be worthwhile to ponder that if everybody were to place a bet on whether they are in a simulation or not, then if people use the bland principle of indifference, and consequently place their money on being in a simulation if they know that that's where almost all people are, then almost everyone will win their bets. If they bet on not being in a simulation, then almost everyone will lose.[2]

Assuming that, one day, we will be able to create artificial minds and artificial worlds – and assuming that we will be inclined to create numerous simulations of human history – the vast majority of conscious beings who will ever have lived will never have set foot in the physical world. It is very likely that any given person – oneself included – is among them.

Bostrom believes that since we are ignorant of the purpose of our simulated world, there is no point in trying to please its programmer. However, others have suggested ways in which we might try to do this. The American economist Robin Hanson advises: 'If you might be living in a simulation then all else equal you should care less about others, live more for today, make your world more likely to become rich, expect to and try more to participate in pivotal events, be more entertaining and praiseworthy.'[3] In case our descendants' tastes should vary from ours:

one should emphasize widely shared features of entertaining stories. Be funny, outrageous, violent, sexy, strange, pathetic, heroic, ... in a word 'dramatic'. Being a martyr might even be a good thing for you, if that makes your story so compelling that other descendants will also want to [simulate] you ... If our descendants sometimes play parts in their simulations, if they are more likely to play more famous people, and if they tend to end simulations when they are not enjoying themselves, then you should take care to keep famous people happy, or at least interested. And if they are more likely to keep in their simulation the people they find more interesting, then you should try to stay personally interesting to the famous people around you.[4]

Plato first suggested the idea of a virtual world in the fourth century BC. The Greek philosopher compared the physical realm to a cave in which people were chained, their backs to the entrance. Having spent their entire lives able to see only the shadows cast on to the far wall of their prison by people walking past the cave, they mistake these flickering shapes for real human beings. According to Plato, our everyday perceptions work in the same way, in that we see around us only the shifting reflections of a higher realm. There could be no question of having 'knowledge' of the physical world since we can only truly *know*, he argued, that which was truly real. 'Truly real' objects were eternal and unchanging, rather like numbers or a concept such as 'Gold', which was to be distinguished from imperfect worldly instances of gold. The plane in which these perfect entities resided was beyond the reach of our eyes and ears. Nonetheless, Plato promised that it could be explored with the power of reason. The French philosopher René Descartes put out a similar message in the seventeenth century. He imagined a 'Malicious Demon', who was able to construct an entirely fictitious environment around us, such that our every belief would be mistaken. Reason could again come to our aid: if we could only establish the existence of God as a necessary truth, then this kernel of knowledge would underwrite our everyday beliefs about the world around us. Descartes thought that any sufficiently 'clear and distinct' perception would have to be true because, unlike the demon, the Almighty would not lead us astray in those beliefs that he seems so eager to press upon us. Unsurprisingly, it proved no easier to demonstrate beyond doubt the existence of God than the existence of tables and chairs. Plato's 'higher realm' too is the subject of speculation, rather than an object of knowledge.

In 1787, Immanuel Kant wrote that 'it still remains a scandal to philosophy and to human reason in general that the existence of things outside us ... must be accepted merely *on faith*, and that if anyone thinks good to doubt their existence, we are unable to counter his doubts by any satisfactory proof'.[5] Two centuries later, this 'scandal' has still not been resolved, but it can be said that philosophical society has become more permissive since Kant's day. The ever-present possibility of error is no longer counted as enough by itself to threaten our claims to possess knowledge. Although philosophers still cannot prove that 'scepticism' is false, and that the external world is real rather than an illusion, they have demonstrated that knowledge is at least possible. Most of them no longer seek indubitable foundations, such as the existence of God, upon which to rebuild the superstructure of our understanding. To lower our expectations in this way is not a calamitous defeat if we overcome the notion that in order to be said to know something, we must also know that we know it. It was this assumption that led philosophers on a fruitless search lasting 2,500 years.

Plato set the rules for the chase with his 'tripartite' account of knowledge. He demanded, first, that the proposition in question be true; second, that one believes it; and, third, that one can provide a justification for one's belief. The last condition was necessary to differentiate real knowledge from mere 'true belief' – that is, an unsupported opinion that happens to be correct. Knowledge cannot be left to fortune, and nor can we allow the truth to be attained by a lucky guess. True belief resembles knowledge and in many cases can be just as useful as the real thing, but Plato argued that it lacks the stabilizing anchor that justification provides. This instability was demonstrated in the conduct of the political leader Anytus. Although he shared with Plato's teacher Socrates a dislike of the paid gurus known as 'sophists', unlike Socrates, he was unable to give any good reasons for his opinion. Anytus' suspicions were correct and protected his purse from the sophists' charlatanry, but ultimately they were based on prejudice. Because his judgements of character were irrational they were unreliable, and they eventually led him to indict Socrates for corruption of the young and condemn the philosopher to death. According to Plato, beliefs held without reason tend to behave like the statues of Daedalus, which were so lifelike that they ran away in the night. Plato was concerned with 'locking' the truth into place. To achieve this, the mental state of possessing knowledge needed to mirror its objects: just as they were eternal, perfect and unchanging, our knowledge of them had to be unshakeable and beyond revision. The problem then was deciding what exactly constitutes a good enough justification to *know* something to be true.

Unfortunately, beliefs are frequently true purely by chance, even if they are justified. Imagine that I am waiting for the results of the 2004 US presidential election and see a television news announcer declare victory for 'George Bush'. I therefore believe that the Republican candidate has won the election, and indeed he has. But, unbeknownst to me, when I switched on the news channel it was actually running an old video of George Bush Sr's victory in 1988. My belief in Bush Jr's victory is both true and justified, but since it is also the result of an accidental misperception it cannot be counted as knowledge. To use a different example, I possess a wristwatch that has always told the correct time. One afternoon I look at it and see that it is half past four. It is indeed half past four, and my belief to that effect is true, as well as being justified by recourse to my timepiece. However, the watch is in fact broken, having stopped at 4.30 that morning, and it was pure chance that I next checked it at precisely 4.30 in the afternoon. I have a justified true belief about what time of day it is, but it would be odd to describe this as knowledge, since after looking at my watch I would have believed the time to be half past four whatever the real time was.[6]

We might counter that these beliefs could not really have been justified all along, since our reasons for holding them proved to be fallible. But if we take away the subjective character of justifications and demand that they always deliver veracity then we will be left knowing nothing at all, since we very rarely possess indubitable evidence for our beliefs. The problem with all accounts of justification is that they concern the relationship between oneself and one's beliefs, whereas what we need is an account of the connection between one's beliefs and the worldly facts. Ever more elaborate justifications might make us feel more secure about our beliefs, but that is no good if they are not true. The American philosopher Alvin Goldman argued that knowledge depends both on what goes on in the head and on its relationship – its causal relationship – to what goes on in the world. He argued that if we want to bring the concept of knowledge within the remit of the natural sciences, so that it sits alongside such well-understood quantities as tables, genes, colours and temperatures, then we should view knowledge as a natural relationship between the external world and the knowing mind. Goldman has since spent forty years refining his approach to this task, though he assured me over the telephone that he has many interests 'outside philosophy' and listed 'cognitive science, neuroscience, social psychology, political theory, law', adding 'Oh, and sports'. In 1967, he proposed that to know something is for one's belief to be causally related to the object of that belief.[7] Causal theories were all the rage in the 1960s and were applied to subjects such as perception, memory and action. Goldman wrote his dissertation on the latter, arguing against those philosophers who held that the reasons for an action were fundamentally different from that behaviour's causes. He then decided to apply the same thinking to the problem of knowledge. At the time there was a sharp distinction between questions of how to justify our beliefs and what were called 'questions of discovery'. Questions of discovery concerned how one came to an idea or a belief, and these were put in the category of psychology rather than philosophy. The dominant view was that the mental mechanisms that brought one to a certain condition had nothing to do with the matters of justification that the study of knowledge was all about.

Goldman asked us to suppose that a geologist notices deposits of solidified lava around an area of countryside and comes to believe that a nearby mountain must have erupted there several centuries ago. Assuming that there was indeed such a volcanic event, then whether her belief is knowledge depends on the causal process that induced it. If there is an unbroken causal chain between the eruption and the geologist's perception of the lava, then she *knows* that the mountain erupted. Suppose alternatively that at some point in between the eruption and her perception, an open cast mining company removed all the lava. A hundred years later, someone ignorant of the eruption decided, for whatever reason, to scatter lava around the area to make it look as though a volcano had once erupted there. In this case, the causal chain has been broken. The geologist's belief is not knowledge because the fact of the eruption was not the cause of her believing that the volcano had erupted.

Goldman's account was the first 'externalist' theory of knowledge – so called because what turns a belief into knowledge is partly something external to one's mind. Another aspect of externalism in the theory of knowledge is the reliability or unreliability of the mental operations used in forming one's belief. According to externalism, such reliability is essential for a belief to qualify as knowledge. But people may not know the mental operations by which their beliefs are formed, or whether these mental operations are reliable. People often seem to know things without being able to say how. Perhaps a contestant on the *Who Wants to be a Millionaire?* game show has a strong feeling that Lima is the capital of Peru, although they have completely forgotten how they came by this information. Yet they feel so sure about it that they are willing to wager £500,000 that they are right. It seems unfair to judge that they do not really *know* the answer just because they cannot remember that they once read it in *Encyclopaedia Britannica*. They can provide no justification for their belief, but neither was it a lucky hunch. Even where no justification can be unearthed, if the 'luck' comes thick and fast and often enough, one might suspect more than coincidence, for they may have a reliable process informing their beliefs without realizing it.

According to the American philosopher Fred Dretske, and most pet owners, animals such as cats and dogs can be said to possess knowledge – even though sophisticated justifications for their beliefs may never cross their animal minds. If canines do not require a conscious apprehension of their methods, then neither do humans. He explains:

> If an animal inherits a perfectly reliable belief-generating
> mechanism, and it also inherits a disposition, everything being
> equal, to *act* on the basis of the belief so generated, what additional
> benefits are conferred by a justification that the beliefs are being
> produced in some reliable way? If there are no additional benefits,
> what good is this justification? Why should we insist that no one
> can have knowledge without it?[8]

It is no simple matter to characterize the 'reliable' processes of which Goldman and Dretske speak. In the earlier example, my belief in the Republican victory in 2004, though true, was not caused by the object of that belief – namely, George W. Bush, the then Governor of Texas – but by his father's success in 1988. However, the 2004 result may have been the cause if George Bush Jr's victory was what prompted the broadcasters to show a repeat of his father's election. In this case, there is a direct causal chain from George Bush Jr's victory to my belief about the present, yet my belief would still not be knowledge because too much luck is involved. It seems that not just any causal relationship will do. Had I known that I was watching a rerun, then I would not have formed the belief that George W. Bush had won the election, so perhaps we should say that we possess knowledge only if there is no other information that would have changed our mind had we come across it. I would obviously have changed my mind about the time had I known that my watch had stopped.

However, things can get out of hand when we ask just what else we need to know in order to possess true knowledge. For example, I might read in the newspaper that the president had been assassinated.[9] The report, we shall imagine, is accurate, but had I read any other paper that day, or watched the television or listened to the radio, I would have got the impression that the president had survived, because the president's aides had been busy putting out propaganda that their boss was alive and well. By pure chance, my sole source of information was the only one publishing the truth. Perhaps I was lucky not to see the propaganda that had misled everyone else, but what if propaganda existed that was recorded but never broadcast? Or what if such propaganda was conceived by one of the president's spin-doctors but was never discussed with his colleagues? In a sense, I would be lucky if this propaganda never materialized. Or what if there never was such an aide? Would I be 'lucky' because, if there had been, then I would have believed his or her lies? It seems that we cannot but get 'lucky' every time we succeed in forming a true belief, no matter what process leads us there.

Goldman's ideas were adapted by Robert Nozick, the man sometimes cited after his death in 2002 as President Ronald Reagan's favourite philosopher because of his view that so-called 'social justice' was incompatible with freedom. A libertarian, Nozick pointed out that any state subsidy for a certain group funded by taxation must entail nothing short of forced labour for the rest of us in order to pay for it. He was the son of Russian immigrants who had come to America to avoid just such a scenario, and from his unpromising beginning as an overweight, nervous boy growing up in Brooklyn he became one of the world's greatest philosophers. Looking like a bushy-eyebrowed Gregory Peck in a roll-neck sweater he was also, by all accounts, the most handsome. Nozick gave up political thought early in his career to concentrate on more abstract areas of philosophy, such as the question of knowledge. He agreed that some causal links were too arbitrary to underpin knowledge. He favoured adding a further condition to knowledge: that you know something if and only if *you would not have believed it had it been false*. One's beliefs must be very sensitive to changes in the truth for them to count as knowledge. Imagine a father who refuses to believe that his son is guilty of a terrible crime, and then is vindicated when his son's innocence is comprehensively proven in court. The father did not truly 'know all along' that his son was innocent: even if the verdict had gone the other way he would still not have believed his son was guilty. His belief was built on faith, not evidence. Under Nozick's account, faith turns out to be a poor method of deriving true beliefs, as it is completely insensitive to changes in circumstance. Faith does not, in Nozick's terminology, 'track the truth'. Even when the facts change, faith stands still.

Nozick wondered if, when people get older and more comfortable in their views, they cease to be sensitive to the facts and their cognitive states pass from knowledge to belief. Even if the old are wiser and possess more truths, perhaps, he mused, it is the young who have knowledge. On the other hand, sensitivity to truth may be measured over far longer periods. Perhaps the laws of Natural Selection have favoured minds whose beliefs eventually ossify, finding this to be the best way of ensuring a longer-term relationship with the facts. Perhaps we might otherwise become *over*sensitive, ending up as nervous wrecks who can't believe in anything. Sensitivity to the truth does not mean fragility. The most sensitive are not necessarily those who are most ready to change their minds at the slightest provocation. The meek will not inherit the truth any more than they will the earth. Being sensitive to the truth can mean being extremely *insensitive* to background noise and other irrelevancies. Where, for Plato, it was the justification of our beliefs that tethered the 'statues of Daedalus' and bound us to the truth, for the externalists such as Nozick it is a natural, inherited propensity to believe certain kinds of things because of our evolutionary needs.

Some philosophers object that an evolutionary process would in fact deliver nothing of the sort, because it is geared to ensuring not that our beliefs are true, but that they enable us to better survive and reproduce. It is on these grounds that the Christian thinker Alvin Plantinga denies that is possible to be 'an intellectually fulfilled atheist'. Alhough he now teaches at the Catholic Notre Dame University in Indiana, Plantinga is a Calvinist who abandoned a generous scholarship from Harvard to study at Calvin College, from where he graduated in 1954. As America's foremost religious thinker, Plantinga has earned two entries in Daniel Dennett's spoof dictionary, *The Philosophical Lexicon*: 'alvinize, v. To stimulate protracted discussion by making a bizarre claim. "His contention that natural evil is due to Satanic agency alvinized his listeners"', while 'planting, v.' is 'To use twentieth-century fertilizer to encourage new shoots from eleventh-century ideas which everyone thought had gone to seed; hence *plantinger*, n. one who plantings'.

With his tall, lean frame and 'chin curtain' beard, he certainly looks the part. Echoing Darwin's doubt, Plantinga insisted to me when I met him at the Notre Dame campus:

> If you're an atheist and a naturalist [someone who does not believe in miracles] then you have to ask yourself the question, 'How likely is it that the faculties which were designed by natural selection to promote reproduction, fitness and survival and not to promote true belief will be cognitively reliable – that is, reliable in providing more true beliefs than false beliefs?' I think the answer is: not very likely at all.

His argument is that under a materialist conception of the world, the particular contents of our beliefs have no causal role to play in our behaviour, because 'All that counts is that the neurophysiology be right – that the right muscle contractions occur, the right neural events occur. It doesn't matter what content gets associated one way or another with that' – rather as it doesn't matter whether grass looks red or green to us, so long as our perception helps us to identify it as fertile pasture. For example, suppose someone in humanity's prehistory sees a tiger one day and believes he should run away as fast as he can. This belief has greatly aided man's survival, but it need not be the same belief as we would have had in the same circumstances. 'Perhaps,' suggests Plantinga, 'he liked the idea of being eaten, but believes that tigers are vegetarian and runs away looking for a better prospect, or perhaps he thinks tigers are cuddly pussycats and that running away is the best way to play with them.' As far as natural selection is concerned, all that matters is that he runs away. There is selection pressure to form a belief that one should run away, but no such pressure that one should run away for one particular reason rather than another. With so many possibilities – each equally effective in helping us to survive in a tiger-infested jungle – it is unlikely that the caveman's belief happens to be the true one. From this, argues Plantinga, 'it is a short step to doubting all or most of our beliefs – including our belief in evolution itself, thus rendering the naturalist project self-defeating'.[10]

Religious believers have no such worries, as God has given them their cognitive faculties so that they might know the Truth and ascend to heaven on its back – not merely so that they can avoid predators and find sustenance. However, it is not so easy to drive a wedge between the content of our beliefs and their consequences. If different beliefs can lead to the same behaviour in all conceivable circumstances, then it would be fair to conclude that they are not in fact different. So far, we may not have encoutered the predicament in which alternative beliefs about tigers diverge, but given the countless number of situations in which generations of our ancestors found themselves, it is fair to assume that they would have come across the important ones at some time or another. When the tiger catches our caveman it will be easy enough to see that the beast is far from the playful vegetarian he imagined. The belief that tigers are highly dangerous, on the other hand, is not so susceptible to reversal. Put simply, true beliefs about man-eaters are more likely to survive than false beliefs because there are fewer opportunities to refute them. By contrast, Plantinga's God could not give us an accurate view of the world by giving us true beliefs at the outset, since changes in our environment will render any comprehensive 'pre-programming' obsolete. He would need to be constantly intervening in his creation to plug the holes in our knowledge. To a philosophical naturalist, our sensitivity to such changes depends on how difficult it has been for our species to survive in its environment. A swiftly changing world may be expected to produce sharper minds than an Earth without seasons. There are, therefore, some grounds for suggesting that if the world were a better place, we would be less well-equipped to appreciate it.

The peculiar problem posed by scepticism in all its forms – from the Matrix to Plato's Cave – is that it lurks in situations to which we cannot be sensitive. We would still hold all our current beliefs even if we were pod-dwellers or the playthings of Descartes's deceitful demon. Such predicaments, if true, would not be truths that could be 'tracked', so Nozick would say that even if we *believed* them, we could not *know* them. By definition, they admit of no means by which we could correct any mistaken opinions about them. But even those truths that we can be said to know must remain at a certain distance from us, since the mechanisms that connect us to the facts and give us knowledge are simply more facts. So long as the truth to which we are connected is external to us, what links it to us will also be external, even though there may be glimpses of the *nearest* end of the tether. The desire for certainty – the desire for an answer to the 'scandal' alleged by Kant in 1787 that the existence of the world around us must ultimately be taken on faith – represents a false dream. Thanks to Goldman and his followers, we can talk with confidence about how we might come to acquire knowledge. But the foundations of knowledge are outside us, just as its objects are – that is, in the processes of the natural world, rather than within us as Kant hoped. It is worth asking what kind of knowledge could be underwritten from within. We could achieve certainty only if the objects of our knowledge were figments of our imagination – that is to say, if the external world itself were brought within us. The desire for certainty amounts to the desire to become Descartes's demon.

the problem of meaning

First learn the meaning of what you say, and then speak.

Epictetus

How do I know what I mean until I see what I say?

E. M. Forster

The Belgian painter René Magritte once created a highly realistic picture of a pipe, below which he famously wrote, 'This is not a pipe.' One would not want to disagree with a great artist as to the meaning of his own work, but we do not always extend the same courtesy to amateurs. When my neighbour proudly shows off his latest watercolour of a cat, only politeness stops me from pointing out that it looks more like a horse. But even a cat drawn so ineptly that it looks like a horse is supposed to remain a picture of a cat. Pictures must be pictures of the things they are *supposed* to represent, otherwise each and every one would be perfect in being a picture of *something*, even if just of a mess. According to convention, I might fail to paint a lifelike cat, but I cannot fail to create a cat *at all*, no matter how bizarre the result of my efforts may be. However, we would be suspicious if my neighbour's 'cat' looked like a brilliantly rendered horse by a skilled anatomist. It would be more likely that he had intended to paint a horse all along, no matter how much he protested that he could not quite capture the sheen of the cat's fur. He would seem to be mistaken about not only the results

on the canvas, but also the contents of his own thoughts that led to such results.

This kind of error is not limited to artistic endeavour, but also applies to any form of expression – even to simple spoken reports of our experiences. According to some philosophers, we could all be in the position of the deluded artist at times, since our own opinion of what we mean can be mistaken. Not only can we mean to *say* one thing, then, by accident, say another, but we can also mean to *mean* one thing and, by accident, *mean* another. For example, in *The Arabian Nights*, Sinbad the Sailor escapes from a giant bird of prey known as the 'roc'. According to the thirteenth-century explorer Marco Polo, the roc lived on the island of Madagascar. He described the creature as an eagle with a wingspan thirty paces long and so powerful that it could carry off an elephant in its talons. When Kublai Khan heard the tale, he is said to have dispatched envoys to the King of Madagascar, from whom they procured a roc feather. Modern zoologists would dispute that it was any such thing, for there were never any eagles of that size living on the island – or anywhere else.

The source of the legend may be another Madagascan native, the now-extinct Elephant Bird which, though vegetarian and flightless, weighed half a ton and stood three metres tall. If so, when Marco Polo or Kublai Khan spoke of the 'roc', they were actually referring to the Elephant Bird. And it is no use going beyond the words and appealing to their thoughts either, since their thoughts are equally limited to referring to their experiences and the progenitors of those experiences. They are simply not capable of referring to things they have had no connection with. In the words of the elder statesman of American philosophy, Hilary Putnam, 'Meanings just ain't in the head.'[1]

Hilary Putnam was born in Chicago, Illinois in 1926. His parents moved to France when he was six months old, where his father, Samuel Putnam, edited a literary magazine, and produced a translation of all the extant works of Rabelais. The family returned to the United States when Hilary was seven years old. In 1936, 'Sam' Putnam became a communist when, as he put it, 'I saw world-famous writers starving on the streets of New York,' but ten years later he quit the Communist Party in total disillusionment.[2] In the 1960s, Hilary Putnam campaigned for civil rights and against America's involvement in Vietnam, for a time flirting with Marxism-Leninism after joining the Progressive Labour Party. This incurred moves by the Harvard University authorities to censure him for disruptive political activity. Putnam headed off punishment by mobilizing friends and supporters for his cause, but he later admitted that his membership of the PLP had been a mistake.

Putnam is known for holding views on a wide range of philosophical subjects, and also for changing his mind several times during his career. It has been said that this is due to his overarching concern to avoid being boring, but his own explanation was as follows: 'We philosophers are frequently torn between opposing considerations, but we very infrequently show it in *print*. What we do is let ourselves be torn in private until we "plonk" for one alternative or other; then the published paper only shows what we plonked for, and not the being torn.' However, Putnam has never changed his mind on his most celebrated contribution, the philosophical theory of 'semantic externalism'. This is the view that the content or meaning of a term is given by its history rather than by what it presents to its thinker. It is determined by what gave rise to it in the mind of the thinker through his interaction with the world, and not by his or her sidereal beliefs and intentions about it. We do not really give meaning to our language; rather, its meaning is given to us. Externalism holds that the important factors in an act of meaning are thus external to the individual, rather than internal.

In the history of philosophy, thinkers have been less concerned with explaining how our meanings might go astray, than with how they are usually able not to. It is our apparently miraculous ability to talk sense that has been regarded as problematic. In the seventeenth century, the French philosopher René Descartes gave us the 'dualist' picture of the mind and body occupying two separate and self-contained worlds, each able to exist without the other. This left us the task of explaining how the two interact. Our internal faculties of reason and perception are able to give us intelligible and reliable knowledge of the outside world, but we might not have been so lucky. Unfortunate individuals might be born with quite different faculties that cannot furnish them with knowledge. This could be because either they cannot detect certain features of the world – just as the naked eye cannot detect ultraviolet light – or because they are equipped to detect features that do not happen to exist in their environment, as with the light-starved vestigial eyes of subterranean organisms. Knowledge is attainable only where our faculties share a particular affinity with the objects of their attention. The question for philosophers was how to account for the happy coincidence of human faculties matching their environment so well.

An immensely influential solution known as 'transcendental ideal-ism' was propounded in the eighteenth century by the German philosopher Immanuel Kant. While a Darwinian explanation for the efficacy of our faculties screams out to any modern reader, Kant – who pre-dated evolutionary theory by a century – argued that the perfect fit between our faculties and their objects is due to the latter being *created* by the former. He distinguished between the appear-ances of things, or 'phenomena', and things as they are in-themselves, or 'noumena'. Noumena were unknowable, he thought, coming within our apprehension only indirectly through one appearance or another. The character of these appearances is determined by the faculties of the mind that processes them for the delectation of the observer. For example, the colour of a rose is not something inher-ent to the rose as it is in-itself. Rather, it is a function of its interaction with our visual faculties. A creature with different faculties – such as a bumblebee – would see a quite different hue. Even space and time were, to Kant, not features of the world, but ways in which the human mind orders its experiences.

Kant was partly right: we now know that data from the senses are processed in various ways by the brain, and that this processing can take place differently in different organisms. However, we also believe that each kind of creature's faculties are due to the pressures of natural selection. The Darwinian picture, in which a creature's faculties are moulded by its environment, leads to a different model of acquiring meaning. If our faculties give form to the world then we project meaning onto our surroundings, but if the world gives form to our faculties then meaning would be projected onto our thoughts from without. Over the course of evolution, it is our faculties that have been shaped by the objects of their attention rather than vice versa. Semantic externalism is part of the naturalistic backlash against Kant's idea, and Putnam and his followers seek an explanation of meaning that is more in tune with modern science.

Putnam asks us to imagine that Earth has a twin planet identical to our own world in every respect, except that there is no water. Fortunately for Twin Earth's inhabitants, there is a colourless, odourless liquid that flows in rivers and quenches their thirst that they too have named 'water', but it is not H_2O.[3] Instead, it has a different chemical make-up – 'XYZ'. Although a visitor from Earth would not notice the difference without subjecting XYZ to laboratory analysis, and would find a glass of cold XYZ just as refreshing as the water back home, any reference to the substance as 'water' would be mistaken. The meaning of the term 'water' was fixed by the visitor's experience of H_2O on Earth, while, to a Twin-Earther, 'water' refers to XYZ. It seems that the two individuals could have identical mental states when thinking about water and twin-water respectively, yet the content of their thoughts would not be the same. Even before 1750 – when the science did not exist to differentiate XYZ from H_2O – someone on Twin Earth who declared that 'water is refreshing' would have been expressing a different belief to his identical counterpart on Earth who said the same thing at the same time. His belief, despite its intrinsic character, could not possibly be about water, since water is H_2O and he has never seen, tasted or heard about this compound.

Putnam's fellow countryman Tyler Burge responded that, in fact, the scenario did not go far enough, and that not only language but also thought and the mind in general should be characterized externally. Burge was born in 1946 in Atlanta to a liberal family who brought him up with a passion for the civil rights movement in a time and place where it was not exactly fashionable. He came to his métier late. Angered by the prolongation of the Vietnam War, he first worked on the congressional campaigns of Andrew Young, the first black congressman from Georgia, who eventually became Carter's Ambassador to the UN. Burge was then offered a job by Young in Washington, but turned it down in order to study philosophy. Tall and serene, Burge told me that he had no regrets, believing that he has 'made the world better through teaching – less broadly than the political process, but more personally'.

According to Putnam, the meaning of a term is determined by something outside the mind. To Burge, what is actually in the mind is determined by something outside it. He argues that since mental states and acts are individuated partly in terms of their contents, then two individuals with different contents must also have different mental states. Burge suggested a social version of Putnam's thought experiment. 'Al' suffers from arthritis and one day complains that it has spread to his thigh.[4] His belief cannot be true, as arthritis affects the joints but not the bones. However, doctors on Twin Earth long ago decided to apply the term 'arthritis' to an inflammation of both joints and the bones. Al's counterpart Twin-Al expresses the same belief as our own Al, with whom he shares an identical neural state, but his belief is a true one – even though his exposure to the term 'arthritis' has been no different from Earth-Al's. (We are to assume that neither has been specifically told that bones are affected or unaffected by the condition.) What kind of thoughts each Al has is not only determined by what is inside their heads, but also by the linguistic communities that form their social environment.

There is an obvious rejoinder to the Twin Earth thought experiment. We could stubbornly insist that the term 'water' refers to both H_2O and XYZ, along with any other substance that might exhibit liquidity, transparency, tastelessness, odourlessness and so on. If it seems intuitively correct to describe XYZ and H_2O as two different kinds of water, then Putnam and Burge face a staring match with their opponents. As with all such contests, it is only by appealing to what the other side already believes that one can convince them. By holding descriptive qualities (such as wetness and transparency) paramount, we preserve our intuition that the content of our beliefs is determined by the intrinsic character of those thoughts, regardless of the particular processes that brought them about. However, this is at the cost of another of our intuitions: that when we talk about substances, we intend to refer to the essence that lies behind their appearances, and that when we unearth this essence we can discover what we were talking about all along. When chemists discovered that water was composed of a compound of hydrogen and oxygen atoms, we naturally decided that this was the 'truth' about water and that it trumped other descriptions. What makes something water is the fact of its having a certain internal structure, rather than our descriptive beliefs about it. If the use of an identical description was enough to make something water, then we would not really be talking about the mind-independent world outside us, but would be making an arbitrary stipulation. Besides, as Burge points out, externalism applies not just to concepts like 'water' and 'arthritis', but also to 'colour' concepts – so the internalist cannot make use of the term 'transparent' in the description he associates with 'water'.

Perhaps stipulation is not so bad. We can insist that 'water' does not in fact refer to H_2O specifically, but that it covers any colourless, tasteless, odourless liquid that fills rivers and oceans and falls from the sky – in which case XYZ and H_2O are different varieties of water. But this is not the way we want to think about natural substances. Putnam writes:

> What the nature of something is (not in the metaphysician's sense of 'the nature', but in the scientist's or the artisan's) can determine the reference of a term even before that nature is discovered. What *chrysos* (gold) was in Ancient Greece was not simply determined by the properties Ancient Greeks *believed* gold to have. If the beliefs Ancient Greeks had about chrysos defined what *it is to be* gold (or 'chrysos') at that time, then it would have made no sense for an ancient Greek to ask himself, 'Is there perhaps a way of telling that something isn't really gold, even when it appears by all the standard tests to be gold?' Remember that this is precisely the question Archimedes did put to himself, with a celebrated result![5]

If changes in our beliefs did not force changes in the meaning of our concepts, then we would be unable to revise our primitive beliefs about water and gold. After all, not all water is H_2O – 'heavy' water is D_2O, where deuterium atoms replace the hydrogen.

In another of Putnam's examples, if I were unable to distinguish elms from beech trees I would be mistaken when I referred to a particular beech as an elm, even though it fulfils the descriptions that I apply to elm trees. And if a botanist were to correct me, it would be wrong to dismiss his expert opinion. The price of having our beliefs connect to the world in a way that enables them to be meaningful is that we sometimes have to accept that one or other cherished intuition or long-held preconception of gold, water or morality is mistaken. In order to have a sense of reality, we must defer the truth of our views to how they fare in the outside world. This same sense of reality also demands that we cannot have the final word on what our views actually mean.

While descriptive beliefs are not enough to turn fools' gold into the twenty-four-carat species, one would think them sufficient to determine that an object is a chair or a table. For human inventions, we might be tempted to accept human stipulation. However, the late Donald Davidson told a story that shows how this would be a mistake. Davidson was born in 1917 in Springfield, Massachusetts, and moved from city to city with his family as his engineer father looked for work. His formal education did not begin until the age of nine, when the Davidsons settled in Staten Island. He made up for this by studying English, comparative literature and classics at Harvard before combining a philosophy course with business studies and writing radio scripts for the crime serial *Big Town*, starring Edward G. Robinson. He died aged eighty-six in 2003, never having published a book. His influence on twentieth-century philosophy stems from a number of brief papers penned in the 1960s and 1970s, one of which introduced the story of the Swampman, which is among the more far-fetched thought experiments in a discipline notorious for far-fetched thought experiments. He wrote:

> Suppose lightning strikes a dead tree in a swamp; I am standing
> nearby. My body is reduced to its elements, while entirely by

coincidence (and out of different molecules) the tree is turned into my physical replica. My replica, the Swampman, moves exactly as I did; according to its nature it departs the swamp, encounters and seems to recognize my friends, and appears to return their greetings in English. It moves into my house and seems to write articles on radical interpretation. No one can tell the difference ... But there is a difference. My replica can't recognize my friends; it can't *re*cognize anything, since it never cognized anything in the first place. It can't know my friends' names (though of course it seems to), it can't remember my house, for example, since the sound 'house' it makes was not learned in a context that would give it the right meaning – or any meaning at all. Indeed, I don't see how my replica can be said to mean anything by the sounds it makes, nor to have any thoughts.[6]

This might sound a rather cruel way of talking about the unfortunate Swampman. If a scientist transmutes lead into gold with an atom-smasher, as is now possible, the end product is gold – it is not 'really' lead in some way. So, on the same basis, we can ask why the Swampman should not be a real man. The point is that there is more to meaning than form, no matter how closely that form resembles meaningful language. The utterances of Swampman can be compared to an image carved into sandstone by the wind, or a message spelled out by chance in the bodies of marching ants. Perhaps somewhere in the world there is a rock that has been so fashioned by wind and water over the millennia that it looks just like an armchair. But despite its descriptive attributes it would not be a chair – not even an uncomfortable one. What is required is the right kind of history. In Swampman's case, this means the learning experiences that gave

Davidson his concepts, and the meetings that introduced him to his friends. If Swampman is an exact replica of the philosopher, we may allow that he has pseudo-memories of these events and a consciousness of his own, but though he may have pains and itches, he cannot have the kind of directed states of consciousness that meaningfulness requires.

The philosopher Ruth Millikan adds that neither would the being have a 'liver', 'heart', 'eyes' or 'brain', for these categories, along with 'idea', 'belief' and 'intention', are ultimately defined by their functions – by reference to evolutionary history, rather than to their present constitution or disposition. She writes:

> Were this not so, there could not be *malformed* hearts or *non-functioning* hearts nor could there be *confused* ideas or *empty* ideas or *false* beliefs, etc. Ideas, beliefs, and intentions are not such because of what they do or could do. They are such because of what they are, given the context of their history, *supposed* to do and of how they are supposed to do it.[7]

To call the Swampman's heart healthy or malformed, or his beliefs true or false, would be just as inappropriate as correcting the spelling and grammar of the marching ants.

This raises the question as to how much of our own mental life lacks the proper history to qualify as meaningful. Since Descartes, self-knowledge has been thought of as a free gift. We supposedly stand in a privileged relation to ourselves, able to understand the contents of our own mind better than anyone else can, for it is something we can hardly be mistaken about. But if externalism is correct then we can be very mistaken, as self-knowledge cannot be attained through introspection alone. The meaning of our own thoughts is not given to us by their character taken in isolation, but partly in their relations to our environment, and the environment might surprise us. For example, introspection told Marco Polo that he was talking about the 'roc', but his history and environment tell us that he was not. This is not to say that he did not know how to describe his thoughts, which he could say were about a giant eagle that ate elephants, but there was more to them than this. The environment in which our thoughts acquire their meaning is the natural world and, as Millikan points out, this is not a place that is typically mindful of our intentions. 'The vast majority of individual animals die before reproducing. It would be very surprising if the biological purposes of human *thought* were invariably achieved.'[8]

Externalism promises that philosophical problems are more than just disputes over words or arbitrary definitions, because definitions can be settled through advances in science – such as when botanists discovered that the lily was in a different phylum from orchids, despite their superficial resemblance. However, this opportunity for knowledge is also a demand for experience. Imagine that someone boasts an array of strongly held moral beliefs, all of which are united by the distaste aroused in him if any one of these beliefs is contravened. The 'Yuk Factor' is his moral Geiger counter, as he takes revulsion to be the correct and appropriate reaction to anything contrary to the will of God. But he needs more than this indication, even though Leon Kass, the head of President George W. Bush's Council on Bioethics, regards the Yuk Factor as 'the emotional expression of deep wisdom, beyond reason's power fully to articulate it'.[9] In the moral sphere we may be in the position of the chemists of 1750 – able to refer to water but incapable of distinguishing it from other compounds such as XYZ. We may be uninformed of morality's essence, be it God's will or the evolutionary basis of social mores. If someone is actually referring to God's will when they describe, say, abortion as 'evil', then they cannot really mean what they say unless they have in fact been touched by the Almighty. If they have never experienced the will of God, either directly or vicariously, then they cannot be capable of referring to Him. On the other hand, should someone oppose their view of abortion, perhaps on the grounds that the essence of morality is not the will of God but personal taste, then such an opponent would be making the same mistake as someone who insisted that the oceans on Putnam's Twin Earth were composed of 'another kind of water'.

If our beliefs are connected with the external world, then they are never wholly within the province of one's mind. We do not possess final authority over the meaning of our concepts because that prerogative rests with the causal history of their formation. Were it otherwise, we would be living in a semantic fantasy world in which each individual was always right on his or her own terms. Such terms would be worth nothing.

innate ideas

If the soul resembles blank tablets, truth would be in us as the figure of Hercules is in the marble, when the marble is wholly indifferent to the reception of this figure or some other. But if there were veins in the block which would indicate the figure of Hercules rather than other figures, this block would be more determined thereto, and Hercules would be in it as in some sense innate, although it would be needful to labour to discover these veins, to clear them by polishing, and by cutting away what prevents them from appearing. Thus, it is that ideas and truths are for us innate, as inclinations, dispositions, habits, or natural potentialities, and not as actions, although these potentialities are always accompanied by some actions, often insensible, which correspond to them.

G. Leibniz

In the Socratic dialogue *Meno*, Plato related how Socrates drew knowledge of geometry from a slave boy who had no prior training in mathematics. The boy could not produce his own solutions to geometrical problems drawn in the sand, but with some coaxing from Socrates he could recognize the correct answer when it was suggested to him. Plato believed that the boy was remembering what he had learned in a previous existence. Experience in this life, he thought, could not teach us anything of the eternal truths of geometry, since the ordinary, physical world in which we live is a shifting shadowland. Whatever we know, he reasoned, must have been learned before we entered this world of treacherous appearances and moving lines. He surmised that the slave boy's understanding was attained prior to birth in the heavenly realm of 'Forms', where each and every object, be it a horse, a moral value or a fact of arithmetic, was an icon of Truth. Although the physical world could not show us such things, it could still remind us of them. Plato thought that this process of reawakening was what we normally perceived as the process of learning, for, as Socrates asked, how could we recognize the Truth when we saw it, unless in some way we already knew the answers to our questions?

It appears that Plato did not try very hard to solve this problem when he was writing the *Meno*, as there are many ways in which we can identify the object of a search even though we have never seen it before. For example, we may not know what the final piece of a jigsaw puzzle will look like, but we know that it will be the only one left at the end. Or we may have only a partial description of the object to begin with, such as the images of prehistoric monsters that inspired naturalists to mount an expedition to Komodo Island off the coast of Borneo in 1912. They knew they had found the source of the legend when they came across a large lizard – the 'Komodo Dragon' – that had so far been unrecorded by science. Sometimes we do not need a description at all, since the answer is defined as whatever lies at the end of a certain path, such as when we add up a long string of figures. Most mortals do not punch 2,935 x 7,478 into their calculators and then remark 'Just as I suspected' when they see that the total is 21,947,930.

Two thousand years after Plato, the project of discerning innate knowledge began anew. Although many things could only be learned by experience, 'rationalist' philosophers such as René Descartes, Gottfried Leibniz and Baruch Spinoza hoped that the most important truths – those concerning God, His methods and His wishes (that is to say, mathematics and morality) being their favourites – could be discovered without leaving one's armchair, via unaided contemplation. Men and women who have led full and varied lives are wont to accord experience rather more respect than it deserves, while those who have led sedentary lives often prefer to believe that enlightenment can be achieved without all that trouble. The position of the French thinker Descartes, the founder of rationalism, should not be put down to the way in which he spent most of his working life dozing in an airing cupboard or tucked up in bed during his extended lie-ins. Descartes may have been lazy, but he saw that the mind was more susceptible to certain thoughts than others. Show children a distorted triangle or a line with a kink in it and they will describe them as imperfect instances of a triangle and a straight line – not perfect instances of a distorted triangle and a crooked line. We possess the ideas of these geometric forms even though there are no absolutely perfect triangles or lines in the world for us to have observed through experience. In today's parlance, they are 'hard-wired' in the human brain.

Descartes's notion of innate ideas was one in a long history of philosophical attempts to insulate the self from the outside world, be it from moral fortune, environmental influences on our free will or, as in this case, cognitive fallibility. It also held out the possibility of a purer knowledge than that offered by the periodically unreliable senses. This was a picture of a fair world, in which the peasant can be as versed in holiness as the sage, since the most valuable truths are those inscribed on the walls of the birth canal. Moreover, from this viewpoint, it was inappropriate to doubt the beliefs we were born with, since if a notion did not come from our own experience it presumably came from a far better source – namely, the design of the Almighty.

It was therefore embarrassing when the supposed 'will of God' did not live up to expectations. There is an obvious reason why someone would want an idea to be innate – since it absolves him or her of the obligation to justify it. The 'empiricist' philosophers of Britain argued that even instinctual beliefs would have to be checked against experience, as our prejudices are often mistaken. Innate ideas also did not seem to be evenly distributed. Descartes's empiricist counterpart, the English philosopher John Locke, pointed out that supposedly universal truths are never agreed upon by all. Some individuals even doubted the existence of God. It counted against innate knowledge that it was not innate to every single individual, even if most of the heretics were children or madmen. This was not an argument against its existence as such, but it certainly harmed its moral and theological rationale, which was an altogether more effective way of casting doubt on such universal truths. Similar concerns hamper the debate in one of its modern incarnations, namely, the nature–nurture question. The notion of the innate has threatened the equality of all people, since one individual clearly might possess more innate intellectual gifts than another. Once the notion that innate advantages or impediments might be bestowed not by a benevolent deity but by cruel and indifferent Nature was broached, the idea of innate knowledge was no longer so attractive.

Locke's alternative has been found altogether too captivating in recent years. He proposed that the human mind at birth was a 'blank slate' upon which experience and learning made their impressions.

On this thinking, although we seem to have the ideas of perfect triangles and straight lines, the fact that we do not find such flawless figures in nature means that we must be mistaken. As for the susceptibilities to certain ideas that Descartes cited, Locke maintained that it was absurd to suggest one possessed knowledge but could not comprehend it. If we allow that the mere capacity to come to know something can qualify as a form of knowledge, then we might as well say that every piece of possible knowledge is held innately, since I must have the capacity to learn something in order to go on to learn it. There was thus no sense in saying that knowledge was imprinted on the soul in a latent form, so that it might be activated as a child reaches adulthood. This view was motivated by a particular understanding of learning capacities.

Plato had believed that the capacity to know a truth must be very similar to that truth, fitting it as a lock fits a key. However, the capacity might instead resemble formless clay at the outset, which could be given a number of shapes and configurations without tending towards one in particular rather than any other, as in Locke's Blank Slate. No one would say that we have no innate capacities whatsoever – we need something innate in order to be human. What we want to know is to what extent these capacities have content – that is, how much is clay and how much keyhole? Today we have moved on from the question of how a capacity might resemble its object. We no longer talk of resemblances, as we do not think they are essential to representation. Binary computer code can represent anything we care to mention, but a portrait composed of zeros and ones would not win any art prizes (at least not any for photographic realism). While we cannot be sure that brains work in a similar fashion to computers, we at least know that a scholar's brain is much the same shape as that of an illiterate. There is no mental clay within the skull that takes on the form of our studies. The debate over innate ideas now concerns mental *processes* rather than mental states or knowledge.

The empiricist philosophy that came to end rationalist dogmas ultimately created its own dogma, as the need for experience and experiment was eventually put ahead of the results of those very processes. Locke's account contained two components: the belief that knowledge came by experience, and the belief that experience began only at birth. We might well wonder how it could be otherwise, as there are no academies for embryos, let alone heavenly schools wherein the soul might be educated prior to conception. Writing in the seventeenth and eighteenth centuries before the discovery of genetic heredity, the empiricists could not have known that the previous life in which certain truths were learned was not one's own pre-existence, but the lives of one's ancestors.

The struggle between rationalist and empiricist thinking was concluded in the twentieth century due to the arbitration of one man, the American philosopher and left-wing political activist Noam Chomsky, now Professor of Linguistics and Philosophy at the Massachusetts Institute of Technology. Chomsky was born in Philadelphia in 1928 and was still a teenager when he began helping his father, a Hebrew scholar, to edit his works. His youthful support for an ethnic Jewish homeland endures, but he regularly professes to despise the state of Israel. Then again, he doesn't really believe in states at all – describing himself as an 'anarcho-syndicalist'. Chomsky is also one of the world's most articulate and extreme critics of his own nation's foreign policy, once claiming that by the standards of the Nuremberg trials, every post-war US president should have been hanged for war crimes. He began his political life campaigning against the Vietnam War, supporting students who dodged the draft. He shared a jail cell with the novelist Norman Mailer, following the 1967 Pentagon protest, after which Mailer wrote of 'a slim, sharp-featured man with an ascetic expression, and an air of gentle but absolute moral integrity' who seemed 'uneasy at the thought of missing class on Monday.'[1] The description holds after forty years.

Professor Chomsky is famous for his willingness to receive guests, while unsolicited correspondents often received detailed replies to their enquiries, covering several pages. The two guests who preceded my own visit to his office left dazed and teary-eyed after having their pictures taken with him. The same month, Chomsky had addressed the World Social Forum in Porto Alegre on the issue of globalization. A few days after our meeting, he turned up in the newspapers again after travelling to Turkey to condemn the persecution of the Kurds and defend his Turkish publisher from charges of disseminating separatist propaganda. When Chomsky flew in and asked to be tried alongside the publisher, the court dropped the case. It is no wonder that, according to the Arts and Humanities Citation Index, Chomsky is the most cited living author, and the eighth most cited of all time.

Chomsky prefers to keep his political and linguistic ideas separate, and this is perhaps just as well – for while his political views make him the darling of the left, his chief contribution to philosophy was to lay the first charge in the demolition of the left's most cherished doctrine: the malleability of human nature. *Syntactic Structures,*[2] Chomsky's groundbreaking thesis on linguistics, was published in 1957 when he was just twenty-nine years old. His place in history was sealed two years later in his 1959 review of B. F. Skinner's book *Verbal*

Behaviour, published in the journal *Language*. Chomsky's work was a reaction to the empiricist nadir represented by the behaviourist psychology of Skinner.

According to Skinner, the mind could be thought of as box that gave out only what was first put into it via the senses. All human behaviour, however elaborate, was a response to a stimulus. However, the stimuli one could observe and that were cited by Skinner seemed far too sparse to explain behaviour as rich as language. Chomsky noticed, for example, that children have a capacity to understand and articulate sentences that they have never heard before. Nonsense phrases such as 'Colourless green ideas sleep furiously' can be readily understood and judged grammatically correct. He was also struck by how almost all children learn language at a very early age, before their other intellectual faculties are fully developed, and that they do so without being rigorously drilled as they are in mathematics or reading. Unlike adults mastering a second language, children do not acquire their mother tongue by instruction. The very thought that they might do so involves a paradox. When we are unsure of the meaning of a concept, we can look it up in a dictionary, but this would be no use if we did not already understand the concept of meanings. This suggests that our first steps in language cannot be taken in this world. Any child attempting to bootstrap linguistic ability into a 'blank slate' of a mind would be in trouble, for most spoken, as opposed to written, language is relatively chaotic and ungrammatical. It is for this reason that newspaper interviews often result in misquotation – because they would be unprintable without heavy editing. Most parents do not act like newspaper editors. They are happy to contort incomprehensible gurglings into their child's first 'words' and do not correct their offspring in the main. And this is reasonable behaviour. There would be no point in telling an infant how to talk, because they would not understand the explanation.

However, children manage to walk effortlessly through this seemingly impassable obstacle to learning. The Lockean model of the mind presented a general-purpose learning device operating from general rules for associating one sense impression with another. This was in part an attempt to mimic the success of physics in reducing events to a small number of consistent laws. But in the acquisition of language, general learning principles such as induction – where one moves, for example, from having observed a number of yellow lemons, to the conclusion that all lemons are yellow – would be little help if children want to be fluent talkers before they end up in retirement homes. A child is simply not given enough material to work with in order to attain these results in such a short period. Children also learn to speak at roughly the same rate, despite wide differences in intelligence, which one would not expect if learning ability were dependent upon a more general intellectual faculty.

Humans attempting to survive over the aeons have needed a learning faculty that is itself capable of learning – that is to say, one that can become streamlined for the specific tasks they find most important. At a certain point, any learning device worthy of the name will sacrifice a degree of capacity for content, just as, for instance, a proportion of the CPU inside most modern desktop PCs is given over wholly to graphics, sacrificing a degree of versatility for a degree of specialization. Such changes in our learning apparatus are likely to reinforce the needs and behaviour that led to them. For example, all teeth – whether canine or molar – can be used to eat every foodstuff. But if you had only canine teeth there would be a certain disposition towards meat-eating – for the simple reason that it would take a lot of effort nibbling away at seeds with a mouth full of pointy fangs. If what was once general-purpose becomes specific-purpose enough, then it might as well be said to come with its content ready-determined. In our own case, this content is a comprehension of how human languages work. A similar understanding might be programmed into a computer or one day genetically modified into an animal, but for humans language is a free gift. It is also a substantive gift, for human grammar is not the only possible structure a language might possess. Computer languages can express the same propositions as English or French using quite different principles.

Despite the work of Chomsky, the battle between rationalism and empiricism should not be deemed a victory for the followers of Descartes. It would be more accurate to say that rationalism was killed stone dead before its organs were found to be of use to other patients. The dogmas of empiricism were not exposed by rationalist thought, but by a more careful examination of the facts of experience. While empiricism failed as metaphysics, as a methodology it led to all the fruits of modern science – including the new science of lingustics, founded by Chomsky.

The discipline's first steps consisted in identifying abstract grammatical features common to all languages on Earth. Chomsky himself proposed that such linguistic universals were the result of a common genetic heritage. Alternatively, the common structures may have been owed to a shared cultural heritage. If all humans today are descended from a small group, then all languages are probably descended from a single prehistoric tongue. Although the language has changed so much that different branches cannot be understood by others, certain general features (perhaps those that allow for translations to take place) have remained. Even so, humans in unusual circumstances – such as twins locked in the attic by crazed parents – have demonstrated an ability to create a language all by themselves. It is difficult enough for nurturists to explain language learning given the limited stimulus of normal child-rearing. A complete absence of stimulus would appear to settle the argument in Chomsky's favour.

Given humanity's evolutionary origin, some form of innate ideas could be expected on grounds of efficiency. The same reasoning also explains why not all useful beliefs are innate. Although it can confer an advantage in terms of energy saved and early death avoided, even more energy might be saved if such knowledge is not stored innately, because that knowledge is just so easily available to any creature with basic powers of reasoning. Certain beliefs might come bundled with the faculty of believing, but it would be a waste of energy to make noun forms innate if any algorithm worth its genes would soon alight on such a convenient way of speaking. A child needs to learn the arbitrary vocabulary and minor grammar that his parents use because these are not the sorts of things that it makes sense to hard-wire from birth. The more detailed needs of language often change rapidly to match environmental changes, and the slow-moving human genome could never keep pace with such demands.

However, in a more or less stable environment there is great survival value in an innate capacity or propensity. It would save a lot of time, for example, if you did not have to learn how to see the world in three dimensions. As Daniel Dennett remarks on the alternative: 'Skinnerian conditioning is a fine capacity to have, so long as you are not killed by one of your early errors.'[3] It is obviously far better to weed out life-threatening or inefficient behaviour before it has a chance to be tested, although if grammar has a genetic basis then presumably such actions have indeed been tried out and removed from the gene pool in generations past. As Descartes and the rationalists suspected, the most important beliefs are indeed innate, they are beliefs that are important for survival in this world, rather than the next. If the higher truths of metaphysics and moral values are not among their number, we must remember that they were put there not by gods passing their time in mathematics and logic, but by primates picking peanuts and avoiding tigers.

the language of thought

What can't be said, can't be said, and it can't be whistled
either.

Frank Ramsey

If it is true that words have meanings, why don't we throw
away words and keep just the meanings?

Ludwig Wittgenstein

If thoughts depended on words, how could a new word
ever be coined? How could a child learn a new word to
begin with? How could translation to a new language ever
be possible?

Steven Pinker

And the whole Earth was of one language, and of one
speech. And it came to pass, as they journeyed from the
east, that they found a plain in the land of Shinar; and
they dwelt there ... And they said, Go to, let us build a city
and a tower, whose top may reach unto heaven; and let us
make a name, lest we be scattered abroad upon the face
of the whole earth ... And the Lord said, Behold, the
people is one, and they have all one language; and this
they begin to do: and now nothing will be restrained from
them, which they have imagined to do. Go to, let us go
down, and there confound their language, that they may

> not understand one another's speech. So the Lord
> scattered them abroad from thence upon the face of all
> the earth: and they left off to build the city. Therefore is
> the name of it called Babel. (Genesis 11: 1–9)

Philosophers have lately asked whether the mythical common language spoken before Babel in fact lives on unbeknownst to us in the mind of every man and woman – a primordial code, or 'mentalese', into which all natural language is translated for processing by the brain. We may think in English, but there is reason to suspect that English is not the first language of English people. We know that information-processing goes on in the brains of babies before they have learned to talk, and that it occurs when people are actively thinking of different things and also when they are asleep. The faithful at prayer often have the experience of their call being completed before they have articulated its words. With a shrug and a nod, an intention is communicated. Or one can read a sentence not only without moving one's lips, but also without speaking internally in thought. We all have the experience of words being on the tip of our tongues, or occasions when we know what we mean but can't remember the right word.

We need to ask what this pre-verbal information-processing consists in. Sometimes we might think in pictures rather than words, but this would not account for all the instances mentioned. A picture, by itself, can be ambiguous, whereas our thoughts, it seems, cannot. The famous optical illusion of the duck-rabbit opposite can be seen as either of the two animals, but we do not make this mistake when thinking of rabbits and ducks.

Words in a natural language can also be ambiguous. The headlines

'Four Held Over Bomb Are Freed' (*The Times*, London, 7 June 1980) and 'Judge Deals Blow to Bryant Defense' (<www.CNN.com> Thursday, 22 April 2004) could be understood in either of two ways. But the journalists who wrote those words presumably knew very well what they meant to say and could have understood their own thoughts in only one way. As the American cognitive psychologist Steven Pinker writes, 'If there can be two thoughts corresponding to one word, thoughts can't be words.'[1]

Pinker talks of the factor that resolves such ambiguity as an extra element in the head. Philosophers, on the other hand, spent the better part of the twentieth century trying to show that it is context that makes the difference. The meaning of a phrase was to be determined by its setting, which might encompass both other words and the manner in which it is said. The Austrian philosopher Ludwig Wittgenstein argued that the limits of one's language denoted the limits of one's thoughts. He believed that all terms must have publicly available criteria for their use, or else there could be no discernible difference between employing them correctly or incorrectly. By contrast, expressions in a 'private' language – used only in an individual's internal dialogue – would be correct if they 'felt' appropriate, which would undermine the necessity that there be a difference between getting things right and getting them wrong. Without criteria enforced by a wider linguistic community, no term could ever retain a fixed meaning. However, we might develop the same criteria for meaning via a different route if certain features of one's language are common to all individuals as human beings. As Noam Chomsky has established, the basis of language is biological and laid down in the history of our species. If certain meanings were synchronized in the community of the dead, in the form of our genetic make-up, there would be no need for public engagement to underwrite all the grammar of the living, though it may be necessary for some features of language such as vocabulary. Shared human characteristics were essential in Wittgenstein's thought also, but it was our ways of experiencing the world that he had in mind – such as the fact that we share the same kind of perceptual machinery. If the model of the brain as an information-processor can show that we share rather more than that, then the so-called 'Linguistic Turn' effected in Western philosophy at the beginning of the twentieth century, largely at Wittgenstein's behest, was overrated.

The notion of a mentalese, or 'The Language of Thought Hypothesis' as it is known, was introduced by the American philosopher Jerry Fodor in 1975.[2] Fodor was a long-time colleague of Chomsky's at MIT before he moved to Manhattan in 1986 to teach at Rutgers University. Fodor and his wife now live in a corner apartment overlooking the Hudson just a short walk from the Lincoln Center, where he can indulge his passion for opera. I was astonished at his intellect and speed of thought, although the spell was almost broken at the end of our meeting when his wife ticked him off for forgetting to book their concert tickets again. His appointment to Rutgers began a gathering of top minds that has made New York City the hub of the philosophical world today. In part this is a testament to Fodor's status as one of philosophy's few living guru figures. An avuncular, full-cheeked Ernest Borgnine lookalike, Fodor seems too jovial to be a guru, but he has been described as 'the sun around which all the planets gravitated'.[3] These planets now include such philosophers as Colin McGinn, Alvin Goldman and Thomas Nagel.

Fodor likes to use the analogy of computer languages to explain his position. The codes that programmers use look fiendishly complex to the layman, but they are not the 'real' language of the computer. Programming languages such as C++ and Java are relatively user-friendly simplifications of what is required to get desktop machines to do what we ask of them. The real language 'understood' by our PCs is machine code – a series of ones and zeros into which all programming languages have to be translated for software to work. In the same way, it is highly unlikely that the languages in which human beings converse, such as English and French, speak directly to the brain at the level upon which thinking takes place. We certainly seem to think in English, but then computers seem to work in C++ or Java if one does not know better. Fodor also uses the example of animals, many of which clearly employ thought in planning a hunt and solving other problems, as well as in learning, although they do not possess language. Crows, for example, have long been seen dropping clams from a great height on to beaches to crack them open. Eagles in Greece employ the same process for breaking open tortoise shells, as proved fatal for the ancient playwright Aeschylus, who died after an eagle mistook his shiny, bald pate for a rock. Birds did not solve the problem of how to break into walnuts until Japanese crows made the 'discovery' around 1990. A BBC television crew captured several crows waiting patiently at a pedestrian crossing with walnuts in their beaks. When the lights turned to red, they would leave the nuts in the middle of the road and hop back on to the pavement. After the shells had been crushed under the wheels of cars, the birds crossed over with the other pedestrians to collect their meal.[4] Obviously, animals do not possess *human* language, but neither do most species seem to possess any sophisticated system of communication. Yet their behaviour shows them to be capable of complex thought and planning. Presumably, our own ancestors were able to effect similar intelligent behaviour before we possessed sophisticated natural languages.

It might be thought that a richly developed natural language would enable a species to achieve more complex planning than it could using mentalese alone – otherwise we could ask what the point of English and French would be. But Fodor's contention is that such languages were a technological advance in expression and communication rather than in thought. What can be achieved in a piece of PC software written in C++ or Java is dependent upon the limits of machine code rather than the other way round. It would make a difference if natural language learning could change the coding of mentalese. Mentalese would then become more than intertranslatable – it would form partially merged languages. Natural language in that case might as well be the medium of thought. If we agree with Fodor that it is not, then there are ramifications for the popular view that it has the power to shape our outlook. According to the thesis of 'linguistic determinism' developed by the American researchers Edward Sapir and Benjamin Lee Whorf in the 1920s and 1930s, what we take to be the real world is in fact a construction foisted on the individual by the dominant linguistic conventions of society. Most philosophers have never taken very seriously the threat of linguistic determinism to shape sense perceptions. For instance, in the Navajo language there is only one word for both green and blue, but, as Pinker writes, 'No matter how influential language might be, it would seem preposterous to a physiologist that it could reach down into the retina and rewire the ganglion cells.'[5] However, other varieties of mental content might not be so immune.

Modern political correctness is a direct descendant of the Sapir–Whorf thesis. It maintains, for example, that sexist language leads to sexist thoughts, and that the latter can be eliminated by abolishing the former. Big Brother had the same idea in George Orwell's novel, *1984*:

The purpose of Newspeak was not only to provide a medium of expression for the world-view and mental habits proper to the devotees of Ingsoc [English Socialism], but to make all other modes of thought impossible. It was intended that when Newspeak had been adopted once and for all and Oldspeak forgotten, a heretical thought – that is, a thought diverging from the principles of Ingsoc – should be literally unthinkable, at least as far as thought is dependent on words. Its vocabulary was so constructed as to give exact and often very subtle expression to every meaning that a Party member could properly wish to express, while excluding all other meanings and also the possibility of arriving at them by indirect method. This was done partly by the invention of new words and by stripping such words as remained of unorthodox meanings, and so far as possible of all secondary meanings whatever ... A person growing up with Newspeak as his sole language would no more know that 'equal' had once had the secondary meaning of 'politically equal', or that 'free' had once meant 'intellectually free', than, for instance, a person who had never heard of chess would be aware of the secondary meanings attaching to 'queen' or 'rook'. There would be many crimes and errors which it would be beyond his power to commit, simply because they were nameless and therefore unimaginable.

If Fodor is correct, then such a policy – along with that of politically correct ideologues – would be doomed to failure since concepts, however undesirable they may be, are innate and do not depend upon natural language.

The innateness of concepts is the most startling consequence of the Language of Thought Hypothesis. Unlike English or French, we do not learn mentalese, and if this is true, then it becomes a mystery how we can manage to acquire new concepts, since any we come across will be rendered in English – with no pre-existing key to translate them into the language of thought. So if we are to be capable of acquiring new concepts, we must possess the code for them already, waiting inside us to be awakened. Given our evolutionary history, it is just possible that concepts such as 'tiger' and 'man-eating' might have been hardwired into us at some point. But it is less likely that others such as 'satellite', 'Internet' and 'X-ray' could have got in in that way. Fodor's best hope is that because mentalese is a combinatorial language composed of various elements, complicated concepts can be formed out of simpler ones – in the way that 'bachelor' can be formed out of 'man' and 'unmarried'. Such words could be eliminated from the dictionary without harming our powers of expression. It would not be too much trouble to find a different way of saying what we mean. However, this is not the case with words such as 'green' and 'blue', or even 'hot' and 'cold'. It is difficult, if not impossible, to define them without using the concept in its definition – hence the perennial conundrum of how to explain colours to someone blind from birth. This is why philosophers call them 'primitive' concepts. The question then is how many of our concepts are primitive, and the answer, it seems, is quite a lot of them.

Fodor himself believes that almost all concepts are primitive. Because this particular nativist position sounds so absurd, philosophers commonly refer to it as 'Mad Dog' nativism. Whoever coined the phrase could not have had its softly spoken champion's persona in mind, but his ideas, however, are another matter. As he patiently explained to me:

My own nativism is very extreme. I'm sceptical about whether there is such a process as learning. I don't think learning is a very clear idea, and I think as you try to apply it the concept gets less and less clear. I think there must be an enormous amount of innate cognitive structure and information, but this is an eccentric view. My guess is that if you want to know which concepts are innate, ask yourself which concepts get coded by single words. Everyone agrees that primitive concepts are innate. Even Locke and Hume thought that sensory concepts were innate. They cannot be learned. So the only concepts that can be learned are those that are reducible to the basic concepts, whatever they are. What I'm suggesting is that all concepts are primitive. I don't think 'brown cow' is a concept – you can see how that's constructed. But the primitive vocabulary has to be big enough to encompass everything that is irreducible, and as far as we know, damn near everything is irreducible.

Unfortunately, attempts to perform such reductions to basic concepts have been uniform failures. That we can entertain an infinite number of thoughts, understand an infinite number of sentences – even those we have never entertained before – is, for Fodor, explained by the fact that mentalese has a compositional semantics, meaning that beliefs are composed of various elements and have a combinatorial structure. Unfortunately, this was what philosophers used to say about natural languages, and there is no reason to assume that we will have any more success laying down the rules for their elusive language of thought than we ever had with, say, English and French. However, this can just as easily work in Fodor's favour. Neuroscience has yet to come across any symbols in mentalese among our neurons, but neither has it come across the words of poetry that people can recite or the figures in algebraic formulae that mathematicians know, even though conceptual processing must occur *somewhere* in the brain. Fodor explains:

> Suppose that just as you can look in a magazine and find inscriptions of sentences, there are inscriptions of mental representations in your head. They are involved in causal relations just like inscriptions in magazines are. That has to be true if the theory is right. What we don't know – but it really hasn't mattered so far – is what the neurological or physical or chemical realization of these things is. We know that inscriptions in books are made of ink, but we don't know the corresponding fact about mental representations. My attitude to this subject is perfectly realistic with a capital R. If the theory is true it is true because the brain or the nervous system or the soul or whatever it is acts in the way the theory describes.

The eighteenth-century empiricists who denied the existence of innate ideas faced a problem concerning how mental representations were combined to create articulated expressions and complex concepts and experiences, and settled on rules of association as the answer. The Scottish thinker David Hume's suggestions were resemblance and contiguity (or cause and effect). As Fodor points out, 'They couldn't distinguish between thinking the cow is red or thinking red cow and thinking red and then thinking cow because the two are associated.' Fodor wishes to replace this failed model with one of computation. Hume's associations lacked an associator. That is, they lacked an 'inner self' that would manipulate the ideas and impressions to give the desired effect. The hope is that computational values will be able to think *themselves* into shape without the need for such an entity. As the otherwise unsympathetic Daniel Dennett writes: 'perhaps the *prima facie* absurd notion of self-understanding representations is an idea whose time has come, for what are the "data structures" of computer science if not just that: representations that understand themselves? In a computer, a command to dig goes straight to the shovel, as it were, eliminating the comprehending and obeying middleman.'[6] As Dennett adds, one may prefer to judge that this lack of an intelligent middleman is precisely why computers do not contain representations, but to think in this way is to reject one of the most promising advances in all of philosophy. Fodor himself describes it as 'the best research strategy that's become visible so far. If it doesn't work, we will learn a lot from its not working. It's not going to not work for trivial reasons.'

Fodor's theory is the kind of speculation that all Western philosophers traded in before the Linguistic Turn of the early twentieth century persuaded them to stick to conceptual analysis and leave the understanding of nature to scientists. It is philosophy as a proto-science that, if successful, might spawn a new empirical discipline for the first time since Noam Chomsky invented linguistics. If the long-lost 'language of Babel' is proven to exist, then it would raise the possibility that, just as the brain processes the evidence of our senses to make the outside world intelligible, it also distorts our thoughts when it sends them into the world as speech.

postmodernism and pragmatism

Nature, to be commanded, must be obeyed.

Francis Bacon

Ultimate skepsis – What are man's truths ultimately?
Merely his *irrefutable* errors?

Friedrich Nietzsche

Relativism, like skepticism, is one of those doctrines that
have by now been refuted a number of times too often.
Nothing is perhaps a surer sign that a doctrine embodies
some not-to-be neglected truth than that in the course of
the history of philosophy it should have been refuted
again and again. Genuinely refutable doctrines only need
to be refuted once.

Alasdair MacIntyre

Don't talk to me about the post-modern age. We're not
even in the modern age yet for Christ's sake. There are still
150 million people in America who believe in Genesis.

Simon Critchley

Shortly after the September 11 terrorist attacks on the United States,
a supporter of the Natural Law Party reportedly attempted to tender
for President George W. Bush's ballistic missile defence programme.
Major General Kulwant Singh, a former Indian Army officer, reportedly proposed that 10,000–25,000 trained 'yogic fliers' could generate

enough meditational energy to deflect any threat directed at the United States and her allies.[1] Unfortunately, more than the power of positive thinking is needed when national survival is at stake, and it was Lockheed Martin who duly won the contract. Major Singh was an extreme expositor of a common conviction: that if we believe something strongly enough, then that will help to make it true. To some this is a harmless aid to self-motivation, while to others it is a way of life. For example, according to the Wicca faith, Christians go to heaven when they die, whereas Vikings go to Valhalla, Buddhists are reincarnated and atheists sleep the Big Sleep. Wiccans subscribe to the doctrine that whatever you believe lies ahead for you after your death will in fact come true. It would be just as well if something like this happens after death, because it certainly does not happen before it. We all know that there is a link between what one believes will happen and what one subsequently perceives, but there is no evidence that this affects what actually becomes the case. Reality does not take care to answer to human expectation, even with the weight of the beliefs of 400,000 devotees of America's fastest-growing religion behind it. After all, hundreds of millions once believed the world to be flat without this making the globe any less round.

The belief that we can shape the world by thinking about it has been behind the periodic resurgence of relativism. The relativist believes that there is no Supreme Court that can settle the truth of a judgment, but only the smaller, competing jurisdictions of a culture, a society or an individual. The first thinker to espouse the theory was the Ancient Greek sophist Protagoras, who claimed that 'Of all things the measure is Man, of the things that are, that they are, and of the things there are not, that they are not.' Socrates, the father of Western philosophy, defined himself partly in opposition to this view. He noticed a paradox in relativism, pointing out that if no judgement were objectively true, then this would hold also of the truth of relativism itself.

Relativism was given a new hope in the eighteenth century when the German philosopher Immanuel Kant proposed that space and time are not inherent features of the world around us, but rather ways in which our minds order our experiences. This is no doubt true to some extent. Zoologists tell us that different animals perceive the passage of time differently. For example, the optic system of a starling has a higher 'frame-rate' than a human's, so perhaps if we could see through the bird's eyes, the world would appear to move in slow motion compared to what we are used to. Television programmes broadcast at seven frames per second look perfect to human eyes, but to a starling they would seem unwatchably disjointed – as if lit by a stroboscope. The difference in a starling's perceptions is not a funct-ion of the bird's will – it does not 'want' to see the movement of its prey in slow motion, it is simply how its nervous system works. Neither is it an illusion that 'pleases' the bird or allows it to 'live at peace with the world'. Rather, it is the result of the pressures of natural selection – starlings have had to track and intercept fast-moving insects on the wing if they were not to starve. With humans we suspect that matters are more complicated.

However, to say that our minds order the way we perceive the world does not mean that we thereby have any *power* over how the world is. Anti-realists – even Major Singh's trained yogic fliers – are no better at acts of mind-over-matter than the rest of us, no matter how much time they spend meditating. For, even if the world is in fact 'unreal' and created in some way by the mind, this need not make it any more malleable to our desires. As Immanuel Kant argued, we may not be capable of ordering the world in any other way than we do. A world structured by the mind in accordance with strict laws of design over which we have no control begins to look more like the concrete external reality of common sense than the illusory fantasy of a madman or the wishful thinking of a mystic. That the construction work takes place partly within our skulls does not help to bring it within the power of our minds. The point is that though the character of the world may not obtain independently of our perceptual machinery, it nonetheless exists independently of our desires, and this amounts to much the same thing.

It is tempting to divide the world into those aspects that depend upon human observers and those that do not, and then to deem the latter variety more real or objective than the former. The human-dependent phenomena may then provide a window for relativism. But perception is a form of cause and effect like any other worldly interaction. The way in which an armchair forms an image on someone's retina is no different in the relevant sense from the way in which it displaces air or squashes the carpet beneath. Yet there is a long tradition in Western philosophy of privileging the carpet over the chair's occupant. The seventeenth-century English philosopher John Locke proposed that objects exhibit two kinds of qualities that he called 'primary' and 'secondary'. Primary qualities are those that an object supposedly possesses innately, such as shape and mass, whereas secondary qualities are traits like colour that require an observer. So had people never existed, Mount Everest would not be grey and white but would still have weighed millions of tons. Yet something needs to interact with Everest even in the case of its more lumpen qualities and, were the existence of the ground beneath the mountain as fleeting as that of a sherpa's gaze, we would find no reason to make a category distinction between its colouring and its mass. The only difference is that people have been observing Everest's hues for only a minute fraction of the Earth's history, whereas the continental plate upon which it rests has been around for far longer. It seems that Locke's theory amounts to a prejudice against brevity.

In addition to the normal perceptual faculties that enable us to hunt for food, earn an income and generally ensure our physical well-being, philosophers have imagined that there are other ways in which we employ our faculties to ensure our *psychological* survival, to enable us to cope with the prospect of death and the everyday pressures of life that would otherwise drive us to suicide or paralysis. This brand of self-delusion is complemented by the willful misdirection of others towards the goal of *social* or *political* survival. We can think of the notions of racial superiority that enabled the Nazis to maintain power by appealing to the common prejudices of the 1930s, or the belief that a woman's place is in the home. The problem is how to differentiate between coping strategies and genuine perceptions of the truth.

The answer of the modern relativist is that we cannot, because there is no difference. It took the suspicious minds of Kant's fellow countrymen Karl Marx and Friedrich Nietzsche to unseat reason once and for all for a section of philosophers. Although they were themselves masters of reason, the two thinkers showed it scant respect at times. They did so without shame, for reason as we understand it was, to Marx, a tool in the class struggle and, for Nietzsche, an instrument of the individual's Will to Power. Their followers have mimicked these traits – Marxists reinterpreting history to their own ends without qualm; Nietzscheans revelling in the paradoxes and contradictions of their hero's thought. Like individual human beings, truth is for Marxists something that has to be sacrificed occasionally in the service of a higher Truth – the doctrine of dialectical materialism that predicts the eventual victory of the proletariat. For Nietzscheans, the truth is that which crushes weaker lies, and it does so by force rather than via any humdrum correspondence with the facts. Ironically, both figures have lately come to be used as tools to divine a still higher truth, or rather a lack thereof. This is the nihilistic postmodern world view in which 'Truth' is regarded as a stage in history that we have now overcome.

Shortly before his death, the English philosopher Bernard Williams warned that the popularity of this belief 'signals a danger that our intellectual activities, particularly in the humanities, may tear themselves to pieces'. His concern was that the end of truth would mean the end of honesty and integrity, for 'If you do not really believe in the existence of truth, what is the passion for truthfulness a passion for?'[2] Postmodern philosophers would be more than happy to provide answers to this question in the form of ideological motives. Indeed, in the recent Continental European tradition, every philosophical problem has been interpreted as a political question – and one to which the answer is usually some form or other of Marxism. Inspired by Nietzsche, its followers do not seek to replace existing reasons with alternative ones – they wish to abolish reasons entirely and replace them with motives, sometimes Freudian and sometimes economic. That is, they want to replace post-Enlightenment society's leading 'motive' – reason – with their own ideological ends. Reason is to be analysed in terms of power rather than vice versa. However, once authority has been reduced to raw power it is, as Williams says, 'always a mistake for a minority or the disadvantaged party to reduce things to the bottom line, for on the bottom line they are simply a minority'.[3]

If there is something familiar about the continental attack on the Enlightenment, it is because the analysis of an opponent's motives for holding his belief, rather than his reasons, is a variety of the *ad hominem* attack. It is a way of dismissing beliefs that prove resistant to refutation in the logical way. Instead of impugning the victim's religion or sexual habits, postmodernists imagine themselves less crude for appraising his upbringing and class interests. The only difference is that they begin from this approach rather than turning to it as a last resort. For the postmodernist, imperialism is a kind of original sin that ensures that nothing we do or assert is free from the interests of power. The traditional challenge to reason's authority to adjudicate between different people's perceptions was the fear that whim or drink and drugs would get in the way of impartiality. The doubters of the ancient world never imagined the roster of biases that we supposedly hold today, owing to gender, social class and language.

Even the natural sciences are not immune from such attack. The French postmodernist Jean-François Lyotard argued that there were two varieties of knowledge: scientific knowledge and narrative knowledge. Narrative knowledge is the kind that underpins social institutions, values and cooperative conventions, and consists of myths and legends and popular stories. Such knowledge has obviously retreated in recent times in the face of the abstract, more logical knowledge offered by the sciences. It simply cannot live up to its rival's standards of evidence and rigorous argument. However, Lyotard alleges that science cannot crown itself the true form of knowledge without resorting to the narrative form it despises. It is worth looking at what happens when the latter takes place.

In 1999, a panel of botanists called for the common-sense based Linnaen system of taxonomy to be replaced by one reflecting the genetic history of each species that was displayed in its DNA. It was argued that the scheme would represent the true family ties between organisms rather than idiosyncratically human categories. In a sense, this overthrow of the old order constitutes a political move by molecular biologists over zoologists. So long as we all know which species is truly related to which, it does not matter if lilies appear in the same section as orchids in an encyclopaedia, even though they are directly related in nothing but appearance. There is no reason why we should not group organisms according to their shapes rather than their genetic similarities if we so choose. The scientific establishment has judged that the new taxonomy is the more useful one for their purposes, but why should the purposes of scientists outrank those of horticulturalists? However, what scientists were not doing at any point was attempting to change the facts. The revolution they wished to effect was ultimately a matter of mere labelling. Unusual political positions that do claim a substantively different take on the known facts have a habit of misdescribing themselves, for what they offer is really a differing account of what those facts actually are. It may turn out that most instances of political colouring are ordinary subjective accounts of the facts available to everyone of any persuasion, for when a racist geneticist looked at human DNA under the microscope, he would have seen the same thing as any other scientist would. His political inclinations may have led him to dismiss the evidence of his senses, and he may have decided to impute more than his instruments could measure, but he would have differed from opposing researchers in his lack of honesty rather than his eyesight.

Postmodernists have also argued that the matter is not in the hands of individuals and their integrity, for the rot goes all the way down to the very words and concepts we use, leaving language far from the neutral tool we imagine it to be. For example, the late French philosopher Jacques Derrida contended that our values require an involvement with their opposites and that this infects our every judgement with paradoxical 'binary oppositions'. This sets out to be a true theory which we do not yet believe in, but in fact it is a false theory which we cannot help believing in. According to Derrida, the concept of a hero requires there to be a villain, but a hero of the hour can rescue a child from a burning building without there being an arsonist who started the fire. We do tend to look for a scapegoat – whether this be an individual, a god or, via a god, ourselves – so, as a remark on human psychology, Derrida's point is fair, but it cannot stand as an appraisal of the logic of values. The French postmodernist Jean Baudrillard's position is similar to Derrida's, maintaining, for example, that the government sometimes acts like a medieval flagellant during the plague years, punishing itself so as to avoid a greater punishment from God or, in this case, the downtrodden masses. Thus the political system generates scandals that periodically purify the centres of power without risking serious upheaval, rather as the body benefits from small doses of disease in the form of inoculations.

The duality of all concepts, it is held, can have extreme consequences – up to and including the Holocaust itself. The Polish sociologist Zygmunt Bauman wrote that 'the unspoken terror permeating our collective memory of the Holocaust ... is the gnawing suspicion that the Holocaust could be more than an aberration, more than a deviation from an otherwise straight path of progress, more than a cancerous growth on the otherwise healthy body of the civilised society ... We suspect ... that the Holocaust could merely have uncovered another face of the same modern society whose other, so familiar, face we so admire.'[4] Commenting on the industrialized rationality of the death camps, the railways to Auschwitz and the construction of the gas chambers, Bauman argued that it was difficult to separate the 'rationality of evil' from the 'evil of rationality'. However, we can be thankful that millions of Americans, Britons, Australians and Scandinavians found it quite easy to do this. They pursued the Enlightenment project without falling for either of the twin evils of fascism and communism. Contrary to what some intellectuals believe, the world did not go mad in the 1930s – only Russia and Germany did. It is fair to assume that if a hundred-foot wall had been built around the latter's borders in 1913, then Europe would have been a quiet neighbourhood in the early to mid-twentieth century. The demands of rationality apply not just to the means one employs, but also to the ends to which those means are directed. The Enlightenment was a humanistic movement, not a fetishization of rationality without thought for consequence.

It needs to be noted here that any criticism of postmodern thinking runs the risk of misunderstanding its advocates. This is because they tend to express their ideas in inscrutably nebulous prose. André Comte-Sponville, one of the most lucid living French philosophers, has written of this phenomenon that 'Shallow waters can seem deep only if they are turbid'. It is hard not to sympathize with Comte-Sponville when one reads the gloriously meaningless work produced by his fellow countrymen. Here is a typical excerpt from the psychiatrist-turned-philosopher Felix Guattari:

> We can clearly see that there is no bi-univocal correspondence between linear signifying links or archi-writing, depending on the author, and this multireferential, multidimensional machinic

catalysis. The symmetry of scale, the transversality, the pathic non-discursive character of their expansion: all these dimensions remove us from the logic of the excluded middle and reinforce us in our dismissal of the ontological binarism we criticised previously.[5]

Derrida has complained that philosophers such as Roger Scruton misinterpret him as a nihilist, but a recurring argument in his own work is that there can be no unequivocal interpretations of anything whatsoever. Annoyingly, he refused to provide a definition of 'decon-struction', the term with which his thought was most closely identified. At the same time, he constantly complained about the way the word was used, and maintained that the lack of fixed meanings for our words and concepts did not excuse writers from expressing themselves clearly. When in 1998 a reporter from the *New York Times* had the temerity to point out to Derrida that he would do well to follow his own advice, the philosopher snapped, 'Why don't you ask a physicist or mathematician about difficulty?' The difference is that a physicist or mathematician is trying to get things right, and finds that he or she must employ difficult means along the way. Derrida looked for difficulty first and foremost – not because these qualities were necessary to attain the right answer, but because they were a fertile source of allegedly interesting philosophical thoughts. Althought he is renowned for his charm, I am unable to give a per-sonal account of Derrida since he declined to be interviewed, and woke me up with a phone call at 7.30 a.m. to tell me so. I went back to bed and when I awoke an hour later, I was unsure whether I had dreamed our conversation. I wrote to him again to find out, eliciting a one-sentence reply by return of mail: 'Monsieur Fearn, You were not dreaming.' At least he was clear.

One commentator remarks: 'It is always possible that a more extensive or more insightful reading of Derrida's work, or of *Mein Kampf*, or of *The Flopsy Bunnies*, will reveal previously unsuspected depths of significance; but life is too short to give everyone the benefit of the doubt.'[6] By contrast, postmodernists themselves have demonstrated astonishing patience and goodwill, among them the editors of the respected journal *Social Text*. They suspected nothing when Alan Sokal, a physics professor at New York University, submitted a paper entitled 'Transgressing the Boundaries: Towards a Transformative Hermeneutics of Quantum Gravity' in which he ridiculed the 'dogma' that:

> there exists an external world, whose properties are independent of
> any individual human being and indeed of humanity as a whole;
> that these properties are encoded in 'eternal' physical laws; and that
> human beings can obtain reliable, albeit imperfect and tentative
> knowledge, of these laws by hewing to the 'objective' procedures
> and epistemological strictures prescribed by the (so-called)
> scientific method.[7]

Sokal was the perpetrator of a hoax designed to expose the abuses endemic in a certain sector of philosophy – one in which half-understood scientific claims are taken out of context and used to bolster the verbiage of intellectual charlatans. The parody was deliberately riddled with absurdities, including the suggestion that the value of the mathematical constant π changes according to the attitudes of the age. Yet nothing out of the ordinary was noticed until the author revealed his intention. The episode showed that while philosophers working in the Anglo-American analytic tradition are

trained to doubt the truth of incomprehensible positions, their coun-
terparts in the Franco-American postmodern school prefer to think
that if they cannot be understood then they must be on to something.[8] Sokal's hoax confirmed that the refutation of the postmodern
world view is best achieved not through reason – at least, not if one
wants its targets to listen – but through the sort of methods its pro-
ponents employ. Postmodernism appeals to thinkers who respect
ideas more for their aesthetic qualities than their veracity. When their
theories fail to match the evidence at hand, it is simpler for them to
acquire a new theory of truth than give up their dearest insights, espe-
cially those upon which their professional esteem is built.

Attacks on the idea of truth tend to follow revolutions in our
beliefs. A generation of European philosophers took the death of
Marxism to spell the end of the Enlightenment project, while some
of the brightest commentators on both sides of the Atlantic are
people who have repeatedly been turned into fools by their beliefs.
Imagine someone who goes from an abortive devotion to sharia law,
converts to fascism and then on to revolutionary communism. The
simplest explanation here is that this person is not suited to grand
schemes and would be well advised to steer clear of politics. Yet
remarkably often he will conclude that the problem lies not with his
own cognitive powers, but with the status of truth itself. They are
determined not to be duped again, so they resolve to reject the superior claims of any system, including liberal democracy. Thus they
commit an even greater blunder – thinking that they never actually
made any mistakes, because mistakes *cannot be made*.

Given the parade of error that is the history of philosophy, it was
inevitable that the idea of truth would come under sustained attack
at some point. When it did, it was no surprise that this was carried

out by those with 'post-traumatic truth disorder' brought on by years of bad judgement. Lyotard – perhaps the most extreme of the major postmodernists – was once a Marxist, years before he wrote that 'We no longer have recourse to the grand narrative – we can resort neither to the dialectic of Spirit nor even to the emancipation of humanity as a validation for postmodern scientific discourse.'[9] The American pragmatist Richard Rorty has said as much of his would-be allies: 'It is as if thinkers like Foucault and Lyotard are so afraid of being caught up in one more metanarrative about the fortunes of "the subject" that they cannot bring themselves to say "we" long enough to identify with the culture of the generation to which they belong.'[10] More often than not, the philosophers of motive are themselves the only ones guilty of the biases they imagine everyone else to harbour. Their work has achieved nothing so much as self-description. Like those who believe that the terrorist attacks of September 11 in 2001 were part of a Jewish conspiracy, their attitude towards truth demonstrates that scepticism taken far enough becomes gullibility.

A contrasting form of postmodernism has evolved in the United States. Whereas Europe's Nietzschean tradition talks of truths forced into shape by belligerent wills, the American pragmatic tradition wishes truths to be nurtured and shaped in order to help us all get along. Pragmatism is the view that 'true' beliefs are those that work towards successful interaction with the world. As Rorty – its most eloquent exponent – puts it: 'The pragmatist drops the notion of truth as correspondence with reality altogether, and says that modern science does not enable us to cope because it corresponds, it just plain enables us to cope.' Though he is often dismissed as a dressed-up relativist, Rorty enjoys a grudging respect among mainstream analytic philosophers. This is partly because he was once a celebrated member of their school, rather like an abstract painter who has won the esteem of his classically minded peers by demonstrating that he is also a fine draughtsman. Due to the quality of his prose he is also one of the few academic philosophers to have gained an audience outside his discipline. Rorty's books have delighted his readership, but they seem to have had no such effect on the author himself. The energy and mischievous humour of his written work is a source of surprise to those who meet him in the flesh, for he gives every impression of a man in such deep despair that some of his fellow philosophers refer to him affectionately as 'Eeyore', after the depressive playmate of Winnie the Pooh. When I met Rorty at Stanford University, the sunshine, clear skies and the Spanish mission-style campus were an odd setting for a man jaded with the subject that had brought him a degree of fame. He told me that he was grateful for thinkers such as Derrida, because 'otherwise philosophy would be even more boring than it is'.

According to Rorty, pragmatism is not a positive doctrine. 'It's just saying that we don't need metaphysics, we don't need epistemology, we don't need a semantics for natural language – a lot of the things people think is essential for clarity of thought we don't need. It's not a wonderful new positive suggestion. It's primarily a therapeutic enterprise.' It had better be, he believes, because:

> several hundred years of effort have failed to make interesting sense of the notion of 'correspondence' (either of thoughts to things or of words to things). The pragmatist takes the moral of this discouraging history to be that 'true sentences work because they correspond to the way things are' is no more illuminating than 'it is right because it fulfils the Moral Law'.... He maintains that there is

no pragmatic difference, no difference that makes a difference, between 'it works because it is true' and 'it's true because it works' – any more than between 'it's pious because the gods love it' and 'the gods love it because it's pious'.[11]

Under early twentieth-century doctrines of truth and meaning, the correspondence of language to reality was held to be piecemeal, with discrete components of language mapping on to discrete parts of the world around us. This was envisioned as a direct and pure contact, albeit one we did not fully understand. Rorty agrees insofar as using the words and sentences of language is 'as direct as contact with reality can get (as direct as kicking rocks, for instance)'. The fallacy, he believes, 'comes in thinking that the relationship between vocable and reality has to be piecemeal (like the relationship between individual kicks and individual rocks), a matter of discrete component capacities to get in touch with discrete hunks of reality'.[12]

However, getting rid of this discrete relationship does not mean we have to get rid of truth. The late American philosopher Donald Davidson, whom Rorty greatly admired, has written:

If I were bolted to the earth I would have no way of determining the distance from me of many objects. I would only know where they were on some line drawn from me toward them. I might interact successfully with objects, but I could have no way of giving content to the question where they were. Not being bolted down, I am free to triangulate. Our sense of objectivity is the consequence of another sort of triangulation, one that requires two creatures. Each interacts with an object, but what gives each the concept of the way things are objectively is the base line formed between the creatures by language. The fact that they share a concept of truth alone makes sense of the claim that they have beliefs, that they are able to assign objects a place in the public world.[13]

It seems that objectivity could be something like a three-dimensional image of the world formed out of the two-dimensional visual representations that are given by our eyes. It means that to know something 'objectively' is similar to simply *knowing more about it* in the ordinary way. The objective world is the normal world, and not some heavenly realm.

There are echoes of Davidson's point in the following passage by Rorty:

The ideas of 'discovering the intrinsic nature of physical reality' and of 'clarifying our unconditional moral obligations' are equally distasteful to pragmatists, because both presuppose the existence of something non-relational, something exempt from the vicissitudes of time and history, something unaffected by changing human interests and needs. Both ideas are to be replaced, pragmatists think, by metaphors of width rather than height or depth. Scientific progress is a matter of integrating more and more data into a coherent web of belief ... It is not a matter of penetrating appearance until one comes upon reality. Moral progress is a matter of wider and wider sympathy. It is not a matter of rising from the sentimental to the rational. Nor is it a matter of appealing from lower, possibly corrupt, local courts to a higher court which administers ahistorical, incorruptible, transcultural moral law.[14]

However, Davidson's triangulation does involve a component outside the minds of human observers working together – namely, the external world. And it is no less external, no less real, for our relationship with it being holistic rather than piecemeal.

It is important to Rorty that the world is not written in a language, as it were, let alone *our* language, as there can then be no question of getting our language to correspond with that of the world. We get the impression from Rorty that the scientific dream is less one of describing Nature and knowing her mysteries than of reproducing her, being *like* her, making the internal life an analogy of the external. Whatever science achieves will be written in a language that humans have created, but this is no great impediment to objectivity, any more than the fact that my words are words, rather than suns, planets and orbits, would be an impediment to my describing the motion of the solar system. We might think that something is lost if our thoughts do not resemble the world, but only pertain to it. But what matters is that the relationship between mind and world, or language and world, bears up – that is, that it results in reliably successful action.

However, there seem to be truths that have no bearing on our actions, successful or otherwise. When I spoke to Rorty in his office at Stanford, I asked him whether his ideas implied that there is no truth about the way the world was before humans existed. He replied:

> We know exactly what it was like. It was full of mountains and dinosaurs and things like that. But the philosophical question about this is 'Were there really mountains and dinosaurs or is this just a human way of talking about what there was?' and this seems

to me a truly stupid question, because nothing could ever be relevant to its solution and nothing would ever turn on the answer to it.

Unfortunately, much seems to turn on the answer for certain individuals, such as Christian fundamentalists who believe the world to be only 4,000 years old. 'People who believe that have an alternative story to tell of how we got here,' Rorty explained, 'and I don't think that philosophers are any help in deciding between creationism and Darwin. You don't need a philosopher to find inconsistencies in the creationist viewpoint. The creationist account is so bad that any fool can spot inconsistencies.' It seems that it is only specifically *philosophical* truth that Rorty has no time for, in which case the scientists who find his views absurd might be rather likely to agree with him once they had overcome their initial revulsion. If the crux of Rorty's attack is that philosophy is irrelevant, then no one need worry about it too much other than professional philosophers.

What we do need to worry about is the implication that if our words terminate not in objects of reference but in more language, then language is a castle in the sky. But the foundations of language are commonly thought to be the moments when the world meets or confounds our expectations. If you prick a postmodern philosopher he will bleed, and if you kill him he will die – whether or not he agrees with your interpretation of killing. The notion that meanings depend only and always upon other meanings, rather than ever penetrating through to a world to which they refer, finds a parallel in the work of the anthropologist Albert Kroebner. 'Heredity cannot be allowed to have any part in history,' Kroebner wrote, 'since every event in human history is conditioned by other environmental events and never by what particular people are like innately.'[15] Kroebner cannot be correct because environmental events such as floods and famines, booms and depressions could have no purchase if people were nothing but their vessels. Even if we are in their grip, it will be because our nature finds them irresistible, and this nature will be something that is innate. Similarly, language needs a foothold in the world to get started – a point where it connects faithfully with the facts – or it would never have achieved ubiquity.

I asked Rorty what could allow us to 'get things right'. That is to say, how does the pragmatic success of a belief not inevitably terminate in a truth. 'We have a synthetic vocabulary that allows us to, as it were, move back and forth between vocabularies,' he explained. 'We are able to see how things hang together in a way that we weren't before. You can put it as "Now we have arrived at Truth" if you want to, but it's just a way of patting yourself on the back.' I enquired if this was a yes or a no, but he insisted that:

> It's a way of saying that it doesn't much matter if you call it the quest for Truth or you don't. What matters is that a certain social function is being fulfilled. The vocabulary of getting more accurate mental representations which correspond more closely to reality and, as they do, bring us closer to the Truth is a set of metaphors that have outlived their usefulness. It isn't that they're false, its just a somewhat antique, puzzle-generating way of putting this thing.

I protested that most scientists believed in Truth and Reality nonetheless. 'And most people believe that morality expresses the will of God too. It's just a way of patting yourself on the back by saying "I not only have the following views on how to live, but they're *God's* too. I'm not only looking for theories that solve more problems than other theories, I'm looking for *Truth*."' As he once wrote:

> The trouble with aiming at truth is that you would not know when you had reached it, even if you had in fact reached it. But you *can* aim at ever more justification, the assuagement of ever more doubt. Analogously, you cannot aim at 'doing what is right', because you will never know whether you have hit the mark. Long after you are dead, better-informed and more sophisticated people may judge your action to have been a tragic mistake, just as they may judge your scientific belief intelligible only by reference to an obsolete paradigm. But you *can* aim at ever more sensitivity to pain, and ever greater satisfaction of ever more various needs.[16]

The only trouble with needs is that those of one group may be different from those of another. However, Rorty has only contempt for the brand of cosmopolitanism that excuses theocracy and dictatorship by explaining that human rights are all very well for Eurocentric cultures, but that 'an efficient secret police, with subservient judges, professors, and journalists at its disposal, in addition to prison guards and torturers, is better suited to the needs of other cultures'. He hopes for a universal human community, but does not think that the way to go about achieving this is to preserve the elements of every intellectual tradition and all the intuitions anyone has ever had.

> It is not to be achieved by an attempt at commensuration, at a common vocabulary that isolates the common human essence of Achilles and the Buddha, Lavoisier and Derrida. Rather, it is to be reached, if at all, by acts of making rather than of finding – by

poetic rather than Philosophical achievement. The culture that will transcend, and thus unite, East and West, or the Earthlings and the Galactics, is not likely to be the one that does equal justice to each, but one that looks back on both with the amused condescension typical of later generations looking back at their ancestors.[17]

This kind of 'wait and see' approach to relative values is the best one in everyday life. For example, teenagers often prefer the derivative pop music of the charts to that of the 'great' artists, but often they will eventually come round to Mozart or Marvin Gaye should they take the time to listen to them.

According to Rorty, playing off various vocabularies and cultures against one another produces 'new and better' ways of talking and acting. By 'better' he does not mean that they are superior according to some pre-agreed standard, but that they come to 'seem' clearly better than what preceded them.[18] However, one would think that that 'seeming' could be unpacked. Part of the change often involves wanting to say, at the later stage, that we have now realized what the standard was all along, and that our prior beliefs were mistaken – whether that means the embarrassment of remembering how good we thought we looked in flared trousers, how naive we were to argue for a 90 per cent top rate of income tax, or how heartless we were for not caring about animal welfare. It is not as though the changes our outlook undergoes are mystical experiences.

Something akin to mystical experiences were precisely what the philosopher of science Thomas Kuhn had in mind in *The Structure of Scientific Revolutions*. The physicist Max Planck once wrote that 'A new scientific truth does not triumph by convincing its opponents and making them see the light, but rather because its opponents eventually die, and a new generation grows up that is familiar with it.'[19] Echoing this remark, Kuhn argued that science does not progress gradually as new facts are steadily uncovered, but rather by means of revolutions that he called 'paradigm shifts'. Inquiry periodically reaches a point of rupture in which a new paradigm – or ruling idea – is found to be incomprehensible in the conceptual scheme of its predecessor, whereupon a new framework of ideas, be it Newton's laws, relativity or quantum mechanics, is imposed upon the facts at hand. To Kuhn there was no pre-scientific über-scheme that stood outside both paradigms and could be used to pronounce the new one the winner. There are two ways the constructive person can go from here. Either we say that the move has already been made, or that it does not have to be made – in other words, either the new paradigm is not, in fact, radically new and can be understood perfectly well by its predecessors, or that it has some other way of forcing itself upon the scientific community. As Martha Nussbaum remarked, Aristotle was an intelligent man and would have no trouble understanding modern science were he alive today. Having written one of the best-selling philosophy books of all time, Kuhn recanted his views before he died.

Like many contemporary philosophers, Rorty is eager for his work to be sanctioned by Charles Darwin. He writes:

> Inquiry and justification are activities we language users cannot help engaging in; we do not need a goal called 'truth' to help us do so, any more than our digestive organs need a goal called 'health' to set them to work. Language users can no more help justifying their beliefs and desires to one another than stomachs can help grinding up foodstuffs … There would only be a 'higher' aim of enquiry

called 'truth' if there were such a thing as ultimate justification – justification before God, or before the tribunal of reason, as opposed to any merely human audience. But, given a Darwinian picture of the world, there can be no such tribunal ... if Darwin is right, we can no more make sense of the idea of such a tribunal than we can make sense of the idea that biological evolution has an aim.[20]

Just because there is no courtroom and no attorney general, this does not mean that we can neither be guilty nor innocent, but it does mean that there is nowhere for the concept of Truth to have a human use. But we know that such a courtroom must exist, since the alternative is to imagine that human perceptions have the power to change their objects. A philosopher can believe in Truth without maintaining that it should be within our grasp.

When I finally asked Rorty if he did not at least believe that pragmatism itself was 'true', he refused to blink: 'It isn't true "because it corresponds to the way that *human reality really is*". It's a way of talking about inquiry, science and so on that raises fewer artificial problems than other ways and lets more flies out of fly bottles.' I wondered what the difference was between saying that the hard concrete floor beneath my window is real and saying that I will always hurt myself if I jump out. If you can get law-likeness then why do we not thereby have Reality? Rorty said:

The only difference is that if you put it the first way then some philosopher will say 'Let us think about the nature of reality', whereas if you put it the second way then maybe you can avoid that. I don't want to encourage them. There are lots of choices you

can make that will result in disasters, and if you want to call that
the impact of reality, then fine.

I asked if his argument had convinced many others. With his
deepest sigh, he replied:

A few. Not many. If everyone became a pragmatist, there would be a
certain sense of liberation. Just as the eighteenth-century
enlightenment liberated us to become secularists, I think that the
triumph of views like mine would remove a certain amount of
worry and guilt – 'Am I really in touch with reality? Am I using
objective procedures?' – and would, in that sense, do some good,
but I think we have more urgent problems on our hands. I'd like to
think that pragmatist views have finally come into their own now
but … the world won't collapse if they haven't.

the limits of understanding

If the brain were so simple that we could understand it, we
would be so simple that we could not.

Emerson Pugh

Comparing our brains with bird brains or dolphin brains is
almost beside the point, because our brains are in effect
joined together into a single cognitive system that dwarfs
all others. They are joined by one of the innovations that
has invaded our brains and no others: language.

Daniel Dennett

I'd be as surprised if humans could understand all things
as I would if a dog could.

Noam Chomsky

The philosophical canon is not short of attempts to explain our difficulty in tackling profound problems. To Plato, our understanding
was limited by the second-rate world in which we found ourselves,
and to Kant the limits were the boundaries of our imagination, while
for Wittgenstein they were found in the language that defined those
boundaries. But each of these thinkers also had a constructive
message. With Plato we could use the physical world to gain hints
about the true world beyond it; with Kant we could investigate space
and time by examining our mental faculties; and with Wittgenstein
we could take a step further back and elucidate our grammar. Given
the failure that constitutes a large part of all these methods, it is

surprising that it has taken so long for someone to propose an error theory without a happy ending. Enter Colin McGinn: a philosopher and former punk rock drummer from the rainy English mining town of West Hartlepool.

McGinn teaches in the same department as Jerry Fodor at Rutgers and also lives in Manhattan. When I met him he had just finished writing his autobiography, *The Making of a Philosopher*.[1] The book tells the story of a rebel, but there was little anger visible in McGinn, a small, taut, talented gymnast with platinum blond hair and pale blue eyes. I think he smiled when his cat chewed up my microphone, but I could not be sure as he has the demeanour of a Zen Buddhist. He was once introduced to the actress Jennifer Aniston at a party. Although Aniston was impressed to meet a professional philosopher, the encounter ended in embarrassment when she proved never to have heard of Kant, Descartes or Bertrand Russell. McGinn subsequently agonized over what he describes as the 'interpersonal discomfort' caused to the poor multimillionaire movie star. Jennifer Aniston is not the only luminary he has made uncomfortable. One of the grand old men of British philosophy, Michael Dummett, once subjected him to an angry tirade during a seminar, and Daniel Dennett has dismissed his claims as 'embarrassing'. The claims to which Dennett was referring are at once bold and modest: most philosophical problems, McGinn believes, will never be solved because of our intellectual shortcomings. McGinn's early underachievement in the classroom may have influenced him in adopting this view. He failed his eleven-plus exam, and was sent to a secondary modern school in Blackpool but still made it to Manchester University, where his heroes were John Lennon and Bertrand Russell – a difficult pair to imitate at the same time. Opting for the latter,

McGinn began smoking Russell's favourite brand of pipe tobacco in the hope that it would make him as clever as the man himself. Finding that it did not, he moved on to Noam Chomsky, who was to become his greatest influence. McGinn was struck by the dark flip-side of Noam Chomsky's nativist philosophy – the thought that with innate knowledge comes innate ignorance. If there are things which it is in our nature to know, then our constitution might also bar us from apprehending certain other truths.

McGinn founded the philosophical school known as the 'mysterians', or the 'new mysterians', to differentiate them from the old, dualist mysterians as well as the punk rock pioneers '? and the Mysterians' of 96 Tears fame (McGinn is often mistaken for a band member). His classic statement of mysterian doctrine, *Problems in Philosophy*,[2] was provisionally named 'The Hardness of Philosophy' until the publisher convinced him that a book with such a title would never sell. McGinn writes that there are two sorts of questions: problems and mysteries. Problems are those questions it is within our capacity to answer, whereas a mystery is a question that falls outside our cognitive space: 'it is analogous to the idea of items that lie outside of a creature's phenomenal or perceptual or affective space – sensations it cannot feel, properties it cannot perceive, emotions it cannot experience. If we suppose that the creature possesses "organs" that define these spaces, then mysteries are questions for which the given creature lacks the requisite intellectual organ(s).'[3] We make so little progress in philosophy 'for the same reason that we make so little progress in unassisted flying – that is, we lack the requisite equipment. We have gaps in our cognitive skills as we have gaps in our motor skills – though in both cases we can see what we are missing and feel the resulting frustrations.'[4] So philosophy's difficulty is not due to the ambiguities in our conceptual scheme or the intricacy of its questions, nor is it a result of the meaninglessness of those questions – it is a simple matter of physiology. It is not what the subject matter is like intrinsically that makes it mysterious (or obvious). The world itself is flatly neutral, but due to the limits of our particular cognitive architecture we do not perceive or understand it as such. McGinn contends that our experience of profundity when we examine philosophical problems comes from a tendency to project our shortcomings on to the mysteries in question, so raising the spectre of occult ontology. The subject matter of mysteries has no special ontological status: 'Steam engines do not turn occult when the possible world in which they exist happens to lack any creatures with the mental capacity to understand their workings.'[5] Many thinkers have imagined a world beyond our grasp, but few have expected it to be quite so mundane.

If there are intelligent beings on other worlds, the questions they regard as problems and mysteries may differ from our own. The answer to a question that to us seems insoluble might be quite obvious to a creature possessing radically different faculties of understanding. McGinn describes these imaginary beings as moving in a different 'cognitive space', just as birds and fish move in different motor spaces according to their physical constructions. However, questions that we find simple, such as learning the basic properties of space and matter, might seem to them impossible tasks. McGinn suggests the possibility of beings that are incapable of conceiving of negative numbers. We can also imagine the perplexity with which the inhabitants of a two-dimensional universe would greet the idea of three-dimensional objects, or how difficult it would be for someone born without a visual cortex to imagine the power of sight. As thinking beings we do have to have *some* kind of cognitive architecture, but the possession of one variety might exclude another. As Noam Chomsky put it to me:

> We are part of the organic world and not angels. That means that we have fixed capacities. These capacities are highly structured. If they weren't then we couldn't achieve anything. What enables them to produce a complicated output also puts a constraint on that output. So for any creatures there will be a difference between problems and mysteries – between things that are within the reach of our cognitive capacities and those that are too hard for us to explore.

In other words, to be capable of one form of knowledge you have to be incapable of another:

> To be capable of becoming a human you have to be incapable of becoming a bee. Of course, if you have no internal structure at all then you're not capable of becoming anything. If you have internal instructions that enable a certain course of development to take place to produce a complex output, then that very set of instructions is going to prohibit other outputs. Then comes the question of how much the range of our cognitive faculties overlaps with the interesting truths about the world.

Perhaps we could alter ourselves to acquire the requisite faculties so that we could solve our mysteries, a suggestion which McGinn cautions against:

It might be that we are so constituted that, in order to have the philosophical knowledge we desire, we would have to be totally different sorts of psychological being: we might have to sacrifice all that is distinctive in human nature, our very mode of sensibility, in order to possess the kinds of faculties that would smoothly deliver philosophical knowledge. And this might be a type of being we would prefer, on balance, not to be … philosophical aptitude might be a trait we would rather do without.[6]

McGinn believes that humans have a natural method of understanding phenomena. This he calls the 'CALM conjecture' – standing for 'Combinatorial Atomism with Law-like Mappings', although a simpler epithet might be 'reductionism'. To understand an object is to be familiar with its component parts and the ways in which they interact over time. It is to be able to take something apart and put it back together again. To understand physical substances such as water, we must be aware of the atomic elements that combine to give them their macroscopic qualities. In the case of human organs such as the heart and liver we need to know their constitution and role in the body. Geometric figures require us to know the lines, points and angles from which a square or triangle is composed. McGinn's point is that philosophical subject matter tends to defy decomposition. For example, our conscious thoughts are made possible by electrochemical activity in the neurons of the brain. But when I am aware of a grey cat, my experience is not literally made up of neurons. If it were made up of anything it would be phenomenal qualities such as shape, colour and furriness.

The physical processes inside one's skull can be analysed in reductive terms, with the cellular structures and chemical reactions elucidated, nerve impulses tracked and an overall picture of brain activity correlated with speech and perception. However, it remains a mystery as to why all this activity should produce conscious experience. And, according to McGinn, no amount of further investigation of that activity will yield an answer. Linguists famously have a difficult time explaining the workings of the innate language faculty we all possess, even though they themselves are in full possession of this faculty. There is nothing strange about this because we should not expect the component of mind that yields ordinary linguistic knowledge to be penetrable by that which seeks reflective theoretical knowledge. So, in attempting to analyse concepts from common-sense psychology such as 'intention' and 'belief' we are 'bringing one mental organ to bear on another, but this may be as futile as trying to pump blood with the kidneys'.[7] There is no reason why we should succeed since consciousness was designed as a vehicle of mental representation rather than an object of it. But to creatures differently constituted, the connection between the mental and the physical may be as uncontroversial as the workings of the heart and lungs.

While McGinn wonders what these strange beings might be like, several of them seem to be walking the Earth in the form of philosophers such as Daniel Dennett and Patricia Churchland. These optimists believe that the mysterians have sold reductionism short. Churchland told me that the problem with McGinn's theory is that one can never know when it applies. A problem may seem insurmountable, but a breakthrough might be just around the corner, and we will never find out if we start dismissing problems as mysteries. An impasse is no evidence for a mysterian barrier. Mysterian philosophy may amount to mere defeatism prompted by the vast expanses of time that are sometimes required to solve a problem. For example, hand axes were around for 30,000 years before someone thought of fastening an axehead to a shaft, even though human cranial capacity did not change appreciably in that timescale. One would think that a caveman chipping away with the same tools that had been used for 29,000 years would have reason enough to believe that no better technology would be conceived, but we know that he would have been wrong. As Churchland once wrote, 'Now suppose we do find some phenomenon really mysterious. This is a psychological fact about us – not a metaphysical fact about the nature of the world. It is a fact about what we do and do not know, about where science has and has not reached.'[8] Though mysterianism is a theory about our mental faculties, these, as physiological facts, are in the domain of nature and as such cannot be determined from our instinctive perplexity.

Mysterianism may stand as a piece of speculative psychology, but it must also fall as one. There are no unchallenged candidates for mystery. McGinn himself picks the problems of the self, free will and knowledge among them – three questions which philosophers have given a pretty good account of in recent years. As for the problem of the mental arising from the physical, Dennett even named one of his books on the subject *Consciousness Explained*. If there are things we are constitutionally incapable of understanding, then where to draw the line will clearly be one of them, as this would seem to require our being able to stand on both sides of it. That is to say, a paradox would be involved in knowing enough about the issue to say why we can never comprehend it. If there is anything we are incapable of knowing, it is whether or not mysterianism is correct.

There are two ways in which parts of the world may be beyond our comprehension: either a phenomenon within our experience is ineffable, or we might be incapable of noticing its existence. The question is whether we can comprehend all that we can apprehend, and there is reason to suspect that the answer is yes. Presumably, cats and dogs do not wonder what the strange inscriptions of human writing are all about. They do not realize that there is such a thing as writing at all, and presumably this is why cats see nothing wrong in settling down to sleep on the newspaper you are reading. As Bernard Williams remarked of moral values, as soon as we come into contact with an alien culture and recognize one of its practices as represent-ing ethical thought, it ceases to be incommensurable with our own value system. We would never think of truly incommensurable values as values at all, if the idea of such values even makes sense. The sonar sense, or echolocation, employed by bats is often cited as something that precludes our knowing what it is like to be such a creature. The American philosopher Thomas Nagel writes that: 'Even if I could by gradual degrees be transformed into a bat, nothing in my present constitution enables me to imagine what the experiences of such a future stage of myself thus metamorphosed would be like,' which leads him to argue that 'there are facts that do not consist in the truth of propositions expressible in a human language'.[9] However, sonar is a mode of representing data rather than a source of data in itself (in the sense relevant here, that is – since we have data that it exists and also know reasonably well how it works). Being excluded from rep-resenting things in a *particular* way is different from being unable to represent them in any way.

One could argue that our inability to experience echolocation is not a philosophical problem at all, but an unmysterious physical problem, much like not possessing a car. The English philosopher D.H. Mellor deals with the problem of selfhood in a similar way.

I might wonder why I am me, rather than someone else, such as Bill Clinton or Britney Spears or my next-door neighbour, and seek facts in the world that caused Me (my ego) to be me (Nicholas Fearn). Because there can be no such facts, my own existence can seem mystifying – I might wonder whether someone else could have been Nicholas Fearn, or whether I could have been someone else, or no one at all. Mellor explains that such enquiries are like asking why it is Tuesday today: 'Once we know what *a* self is, there need be no more mystery about that than there is about what it takes to be *this* room when we know what *a* room is.'[10]

We can ask whether it is our abilities or the abilities of our tools that are supposedly insufficient for understanding bat experiences. If it is our own physical, intellectual faculties, then we are capable of very little once all our tools – our vocabularies, scientific methods, mathematics – are taken away. But if our tools are allowed then things look brighter, since there is potentially no limit to what tools we might develop and use. For example, our lack of a sense of echo-location has not stopped anyone from using high-frequency microphones and scanners to research theses on bat sonar. Neither would anyone suggest that there are multiplication sums we cannot understand because the number of digits involved precludes even the greatest mathematical genius from working out the answer without the aid of a computer. Some tools, such as logic and adjectives, seem so close as to be a part of us, whereas others, such as supercomputers, seem to provide us with an understanding at one remove. Physicists often explain phenomena with highly counter-intuitive theories. These solutions may be difficult for most of us to comprehend – and, as with quantum theory, perhaps no one can understand them completely – yet they are the answers nonetheless. They are the answers because if you do the maths, they are what you get, even if you have difficulty translating the calculations into a physical process that one can imagine.

The Christian philosopher Peter Van Inwagen sympathizes with the mysterians, but suggests another possibility:

> Individual achievement in philosophical knowledge is possible, even though we can't pass on this philosophical knowledge in a reliable way, at this stage of history, whereas scientific knowledge (though maybe not the creative process) can reliably be passed on to others simply by teaching and textbooks. Maybe you can have knowledge, or at least justified true belief, in philosophy, but the grounds of your certainty are inarticulable.

I asked him if he himself knew anything incommunicable. 'I hope so,' he replied, 'though this probably has more to do with God than me. If there were no incommunicable reasons for beliefs then we'd believe a lot less than we do. You might consider people's political beliefs, for example. They come up with communicable reasons for them, but they don't convince anybody else.' The brothers Hubert and Stuart Dreyfus have propounded a quasi-mysterian account of this view. The aim of philosophers from Socrates to Kant was to divine the nature of universals such as Good, Truth and Beauty. If we knew their intrinsic nature we would be better equipped to act in accordance with them – to behave properly, judge propitiously and reason wisely. We imagine that we stumble our way towards knowledge, first noticing particular cases of a truth before realizing the rule or principle that unites all facts of the given kind and then applying it to divine new insights. It seems, then, that we get so used to employing this rule that we forget we are doing so, and when asked about the rules we are using we are unable to reply.

Socrates found this to be true of many experts in ancient Athens, and spent his time trying to extract the rules from those forgetful individuals. In Plato's early dialogue *Euthyphro*, the father of philosophy interrogates the eponymous prophet as to the nature of piety. Like the experts of Plato's other dialogues, the best Euthyphro can do is to give examples of pious acts, recounting mythological tales of gods and men behaving in a way that everyone agrees is pious. But when Socrates lost his patience, demanding to know the rules by which the prophet could recognize these as cases of the virtue, Euthyphro was lost for words. The same story is repeated in many other dialogues, in which Socrates's hapless guest is able to make confident judgements within his area of expertise yet cannot articulate how he generates them. Their tormentor concluded that these supposed authorities were in fact as ignorant as he professed himself to be, but, as the Dreyfus brothers explain:

> Plato admired Socrates and saw his problem. So he developed an account of what caused the difficulty. Experts, at least in areas involving non-empirical knowledge such as morality and mathematics, had, in another life, Plato said, learned the principles involved, but they had forgotten them. The role of the philosopher was to help such moral and mathematical experts recollect the principles on which they act.[11]

However, the brothers claim that Socrates got learning entirely the wrong way round. They contend that rules are only for beginners and that the greatest expertise is the ability to discern endless special cases without recourse to rules. For example, we all know how to tie our shoelaces, but we cannot say how to do it. Yet there was probably a time for each of us when we could do a better job of explaining – at the stage when we had to think very carefully in order to perform this task. Now that we are used to it, we have forgotten the explicit steps involved as we no longer need to cognize them explicitly in order to get the job done – 'Normally an expert does not calculate. He does not solve problems. He does not even think. He just does what normally works and, of course, it normally works.'[12] Thus to ask an expert for the rules he is using is to force him to regress to the level of a beginner and state the principles he learned in school, and with the awkwardness of remembering comes the awkwardness of his early career. A beginner behaves like a particularly inefficient, heuristically programmed computer, whereas an expert acts intuitively.

Colin McGinn has come to terms with what he regards as the insolubility of philosophical problems. He told me that he was as comfortable as ever with his mysterian views. As he wrote in a footnote, 'I take wry pleasure in the thought that [my theory] will probably be the orthodox opinion in the dying stages of the sun's heat.'[13] If the Dreyfus brothers are right, then some of the questions deemed unanswerable by the mysterians were settled long before philosophers got to work.

part three

what should I do?

moral luck

Good-nature, or what is often considered as such, is the most selfish of all the virtues: it is nine times out of ten mere indolence of disposition.

William Hazlitt

Conscience is the inner voice which warns us that someone may be looking.

H. L. Mencken

If Hitler had not overrun Europe and exterminated millions, but instead had died of a heart attack after occupying the Sudetenland, Chamberlain's action at Munich would still have utterly betrayed the Czechs, but it would not be the great moral disaster that has made his name a household word.

Thomas Nagel

One evening, in April 2004, a rumour spread through the English village of Wooler that a local ATM machine was paying out twice as much cash as every customer asked for. The pubs emptied and front doors were left swinging on their hinges as villagers rushed to withdraw as much money as their cards allowed. Within the hour, the queue outside Barclays Bank stretched the length of the High Street and an otherwise law-abiding community had become a den of thieves. Only one beneficiary was reported to have returned her gains the next day. Rather than prosecute so many individuals, the bank decided to write off its loss, and the event is now remembered fondly by some as 'Golden Wednesday'.[1] Given the quantity of culprits, moral condemnation too might go the way of the law. Yet it was wrongdoing nonetheless, and many would feel that those who gave in to temptation cheapened their integrity as they fattened their wallets. At the same time, those who drained the machine did not plan for their local savings bank to start dispensing free money. Their pecuniary good fortune was matched by an equal dose of bad luck in the moral realm. For had they not been presented with such an opportunity, they would no doubt have continued to lead relatively blameless lives.

Philosophers have spent most of the discipline's history denying that any such thing can take place, arguing that although luck can impinge upon our physical and mental well-being, it cannot enhance or discolour our inherent virtue or lack thereof. The Ancient Greek moral project was concerned with insulating our lives against ill fortune. While our material circumstance could not be rendered immune to the Fates, it was thought that one's internal life possessed a degree of freedom from their incursions. Tragedies might affect our emotions as well as our flesh, but at least our *attitudes* to these thoughts and feelings could remain untouched. Our vigour may be wasted by sickness, our solvency ruined by unemployment, but similar catastrophes cannot befall our moral worth. If the latter is debased – or enhanced – it can only be the result of our own will, our own decisions. The integrity of a good intention is invulnerable, no matter what its first contact with the world brings. As Immanuel Kant wrote in the seventeenth century:

Even if it should happen that, by a particularly unfortunate fate or by the niggardly provision of a stepmotherly nature, this will should be wholly lacking in power to accomplish its purpose, and even if the greatest effort should not avail it to achieve anything of its end, and if there remained only the good will … it would sparkle like a jewel in its own right.[2]

The problem is that, like most jewels, a good will cannot sparkle until it has been dug up from beneath the ground. In other words, it needs to be acted upon. Actions, however, can be successful or unsuccessful, the outcome always depending to some degree on external contingencies. Not until the late twentieth century did moral philosophers became comfortable with this predicament. It was the English philosopher Sir Bernard Williams who coined the term 'moral luck' to describe it.

To illustrate moral luck, Williams gave me the example of Paul Gauguin, the impressionist painter who abandoned his family to live on an island in the South Seas in the belief that this would help him to become a great artist. On the face of it this was a selfish act, but its wickedness was mitigated by the success of his plan. According to Williams, the only fact that will settle the question of whether Gauguin was justified is whether he was successful or not. However, no matter how confident in his talent Gauguin may have been, he could not have been absolutely certain that he was correct in assessing his potential. The painter therefore could not have determined through reason whether his decision was morally justified at the time he made it. Since his success depended at least in part upon luck, his decision was a moral gamble. While winning a bet may make one richer, we would normally assume that it cannot make one a better person. Yet as we inspect Gaugin's works in the Musée D'Orsée in Paris, we tend to commend his self-belief rather than condemn his selfishness. At the very least, his additions to the canon of great art prove that his selfishness was not conceit. For the sake of his moral status, Gauguin was fortunate to have turned out to possess the talent to succeed.

Moral luck can work against us as well as in our favour. The American philosopher Thomas Nagel has remarked on the 'morally significant difference' between reckless driving and manslaughter. Whether a reckless driver hits a child depends on whether one crosses the road at the moment he passes the red light. Were the driver entirely blameless, he would feel terrible about his role in the event but would not have to feel morally wretched. But if any negligence whatsoever was involved – for example, if he failed to get his brakes checked regularly or neglected to have a full night's sleep before beginning his journey – he would blame himself for the death of the child. As Nagel writes:

> What makes this an example of moral luck is that he would have to blame himself only slightly for the negligence itself if no situation arose which required him to brake suddenly and violently to avoid hitting the child. Yet the *negligence* is the same in both cases, and the driver has no control over whether a child will run into his path ... If one negligently leaves the bath running with the baby in it, one will realize, as one bounds up the stairs toward the bathroom, that if the baby has drowned one has done something awful, whereas if it has not one has merely been careless.[3]

In Nagel's view, there are legal uses in holding the driver responsible for what he has done, but it would be irrational to extend this judgment to his moral character.

Williams disagreed, and introduced the notion of 'agent regret'. If the reckless driver were a friend of ours we would rally round and tell him that it was not his fault and that he should not feel guilty. But we would also understand his emotions, as they would be quite natural in the circumstances. Williams himself thought that it would betray insanity not to experience such feelings, as we cannot detach ourselves from the unintentional aspects of our behaviour while retaining our personal identity and character. Even though we do not regard the driver as responsible, we would think much worse of him if he felt no regret but just shrugged and said, 'It's a terrible thing that has happened, but I did everything I could to avoid it.' It is also doubtful that it would be a better world if we blithely disregarded the terrible but unforeseen consequences of our actions. As the philosopher Margaret Walker has pointed out, we can rely on friends to adapt to a change in our needs that they could not have foreseen when they became our friends, and we can expect parents to care for their sick children although they themselves did not cause the illness.[4] It is in the nature of duties to often exceed their initial remit, and moral predicaments can foist themselves upon us. By accepting moral luck, by accepting responsibilities that we did not seek, we are able to display virtues that otherwise would not be exercised. For example, by accepting the open-ended nature of responsibility, we are able to display the virtue of dependability by accepting that we will be there for our friends, even if their needs are not in our control.

Some philosophers have used the question of opportunity as a further means to deny the existence of moral luck. Norvin Richards argues that the 'luck' enjoyed by those negligent drivers who do *not* run down a pedestrian consists in their culpability going unnoticed. That is to say, both they and the 'killer' driver are equally contemptible. The bad luck involved is not that which diminishes our moral character, but rather that which renders our poor character transparent to others. Richards suggests that the culpability is in fact worse in the case of the supposedly 'morally fortunate' driver – as his bad behaviour is more likely to persist. The fortunate Briton who never had to face Nazi occupation in the 1940s, for example, 'is likely to live an entire life in which he takes the pleasure of authority too seriously and the pain of certain others too lightly. This will be a stunted life, as well as a damaging one.'[5] Richards's suspicion threatens to shatter a source of national pride for the British, most of whom could never imagine themselves collaborating with a Nazi occupation force with the enthusiasm that the French displayed. Yet, were it not for the twenty-mile-wide natural fortification known as the English Channel, the British could well be remembering a similar experience to their neighbours. There was little resistance in the Channel Islands after they were captured by German troops in 1940, so Anglophobes might assume that the rest of the United Kingdom's populace would have behaved similarly. Perhaps Britain would have behaved rather better in the event, but we cannot be sure of this. Certain occupied countries – notably Bulgaria – persecuted Jews with far less alacrity than the French authorities despite arguably more pressure from the Germans. But, given the evidence to hand, the self-righteousness of the British seems to depend a great deal upon their fortuitous geography.

One of the many luxuries that citizens can afford in the affluent West is a highly developed moral sense. There is no need to declare 'every man for himself' when every man receives food, shelter and security by birthright. With the benefits of property rights and the rule of law, alongside the absence of malaria, famine and high infant mortality, people in developed countries have been spared the requirement to steal loaves of bread, bribe tax inspectors and commit murder in guerrilla wars against government forces or rebel armies. We can even afford the 'moral luxuries' of high-protein vegetarian diets and the animal welfare institutions that inspire laughter or disbelief in much of the Third World. It is obvious that we should not feel too proud of ourselves for eschewing criminal acts that we have no need to commit. For example, someone may eschew extramarital affairs because they are able to reject all offers through iron self-control. Someone else might achieve the same results simply because they never receive any offers. Then there is the case of the individual who lusts after his secretary yet fails to secure a weekend away despite bombarding her with gifts. The wrongdoing of this last character is there for all to see in the incessant love letters and unsolicited boxes of chocolates, but the former two individuals look outwardly similar. Yet while we would commend the first, we feel no such need to commend the second – for we would be praising him for nothing but inactivity. The 'luck' involved is not that circumstances have made the first man a better person than the second, but that they have made it easier to see what a faithful or well-disciplined fellow he is. The second man may be just as virtuous, but it is less obvious in his case. Similarly, it might be possible that the people of Britain would have been the sort to pack off the Jews to death camps the moment their Nazi occupiers whistled. However, in lieu of appropriately testing circumstances, they must be given the benefit of the doubt. There can be no such charity in the case of the people of France and Germany, as they were tested and found wanting.

It would be absurd to accuse people of things they have not done, such as collaboration, just as it would be absurd to maintain that those who did commit those acts should not be held responsible for them, but this is what any denial of moral luck entails. In a way, we 'get lucky' every time we succeed in an action, in that no random event interceded to make it fail, but this does not stop us from apportioning praise and blame for deliberate actions. The point is that although we are free, we can make our choices only from those alternatives arrayed before us. It is here that fortune intrudes, for different people at different times have different options. We might seek to minimize the effect of luck by following a very narrow, self-sufficient path through life, but this is neither easy nor desirable for a fully rounded human being.

This is not to say that there are no measures to be taken. As the American classical scholar and philosopher Martha Nussbaum has written, 'Emotions, in Aristotle's view, are not always correct, any more than beliefs or actions are always correct. They need to be educated and brought into harmony with a correct view of the good human life … with regard to both passions and actions.'[6] There seems to be such a thing as moral competence, which is not just about having good intentions, but concerns such skills as knowing the right thing to do, being aware of others' feelings and never forgetting your wedding anniversary.

Someone may screw up continually while protesting that he didn't mean to, but eventually, after fifteen years without a single anniversary gift, a man's wife will be bound to think that her husband simply does not care no matter how much he protests otherwise. Ultimately, action is the only reliable test for intention. If action is never forthcoming, then the intention is most likely a sham. Her husband's guilt may be genuine in its way, but he feels it precisely because of the light his actions shed on his intentions – 'Perhaps I'm a selfish swine,' he wonders, or 'Perhaps she means less to me than I thought.' At the very least, he lacks the kind of moral intelligence that virtue requires. In morality, ignorance of the law is no excuse. Part of being a good person involves knowing right from wrong. We might deem cruel children immature rather than wicked, but we will change our opinion of them should they never learn some essential lessons. A bad man is sometimes unable to extinguish his virtuous impulses, so he crafts a dungeon for them and remains 'good in his heart' despite his crimes. For this he cannot be commended. We judge a nation by its governing regime and not its political prisoners.

It is important that Paul Gauguin was lucky in the 'right' way when he fulfilled his potential to become a great artist. That is, his plan worked in the way he intended it to rather than as a result of some other fortuitous reason. We would be less willing to absolve him if his sucess was only due to the happy circumstance of a genius living on the chosen island who managed to impart some of his gift to the young Frenchman. But because his success was properly *his* achievement, Gauguin's actions are forgiven and we do not regard him as simply arrogant, deluded, self-centred or irresponsible. An eccentric devoid of talent is a fool by any other name. As cynics have always suspected, morality is, to an extent, about what one can get away with. Acts that would be heinous on the part of one individual might be mere misdemeanours if committed by another. Luck is thus a matter of one's aptitudes as well as circumstances. Aristotle argued that there had to be minimum material conditions in place before one could live the good life. One cannot show generosity without having something to give, nor demonstrate courage without the health and vitality to stand up to one's adversaries. The highest virtues, he maintained, were intellectual and attained through contemplation, but for this to be possible one would need a certain amount of leisure time – as well as the right kind of brainpower.

There is something about Aristotle's account that offends our moral expectations as much as it worried his near contemporaries. We believe that moral worth must be accessible to all people in all times and predicaments – to the beggar as much as to the rich man. We like to think that virtue, unlike other attributes, cannot be inherited in genes or estates. As Bernard Williams put it:

> The capacity for moral agency is supposedly present to any rational agent whatsoever, to anyone for whom the question can even present itself. The successful moral life, removed from considerations of birth, lucky upbringing, or indeed of the incomprehensible Grace of a non-Pelagian God, is presented as a career open not merely to the talents, but to a talent which all rational beings necessarily possess in the same degree. [It thus] offers solace to a sense of the world's unfairness.[7]

The solace proposed by Williams only holds, of course, if the rest of the world's unfairness does not seem all the more pointed when the morally blameless suffer while the guilty reap life's rewards. It may be the case that we would rather have dinner with Richard Nixon than Mother Teresa but, if we do, that is our failing rather than hers. We pay more than lip service to the notion of moral character as the highest value and the real mark of a man or woman. As Williams explained, virtue 'must have a claim on one's most fundamental concerns as a rational agent, and in one's recognition of that, one is supposed to grasp, not only morality's immunity to luck, but one's own partial immunity to luck through morality'. Morality will need to be more important than wealth, intelligence or physical prowess if it is to be the supreme value, for it offers little encouragement if it is merely 'a last resort, the doss-house of the spirit'. If luck is allowed to enter into a man or woman's moral worth, it could not be considered indisputably the highest value, because it would be subject to unearned fortune or undeserved corruption.

The writings of philosophers such as Williams and Nagel are a warning against moral fever. The former concluded:

> Scepticism about the freedom of morality from luck cannot leave the concept of morality where it was, any more than it can remain undisturbed by scepticism about the very closely related image we have of there being a moral order, within which our actions have a significance which may not be accorded them by mere social recognition. These forms of scepticism will leave us with *a* concept of morality, but one less important, certainly, than ours is usually taken to be; and that will not be ours, since one thing that is particularly important about ours is how important it is taken to be.[8]

We may well wonder whether virtue's supposed invulnerability to the Fates was our *only* reason for thinking it the highest value. It would certainly make it the trait that one is most responsible for – and therefore the most indicative of character – but this does not in itself make it the most important value. Immunity to fortune would be of no consequence if we did not already think morality a fine thing. This is just as well, for luck ensures that we never truly control our most precious possession.

the expanding circle

At one time the benevolent affections embrace merely the
family, soon the circle expanding includes first a class,
then a nation, then a coalition of nations, then all
humanity, and finally, its influence is felt in the dealings of
man with the animal world.

W. E. H. Lecky

Me and my clan against the world;
me and my family against my clan;
me and my brother against my family;
me against my brother.

Somali saying

Belief in God, or in many gods, prevented the free
development of moral reasoning. Disbelief in God, openly
admitted by a majority, is a very recent event, not yet
completed. Because this event is so recent, Non-Religious
Ethics is at a very early stage.

Derek Parfit

At the outbreak of the Second World War, the English actor David
Niven abandoned his newly acquired Hollywood stardom to return
home and volunteer for the war effort. 'Young man,' said Winston
Churchill to him one evening, 'you did a very fine thing to give up a
most promising career to fight for your country … Mark you, had you
not done so it would have been despicable.'[1] According to Churchill,

there was no neutral land between right and wrong where one could live a morally quiet life, yet such a life is what most individuals believe they are living. Few of us go to great personal lengths to alleviate the suffering of the Third World, but neither do many of us feel that we inflict that suffering. We are, we believe, neither praiseworthy nor blameworthy. We are not interested in morality – much as we are not interested in politics. However, to the philosopher Peter Singer, we are all as culpable as the young Niven. Morality is pervasive, and by neglecting to do good we each commit egregious acts of omission.

Peter Singer is the greatest contemporary exponent of utilitarianism, the doctrine that actions should aim to maximize the greatest happiness for the greatest number of individuals. Since our every action has consequences that aid or hamper this end, we are truly immersed in morality. With his lean build and exhausted demeanour, the Australian academic seems to embody the unmanageable pressure of this outlook. 'We must follow the argument where it leads,' said Socrates, and Singer – during a career at Melbourne, Oxford and now Princeton where I paid him a visit one wet day in spring – has obeyed this advice at the expense of tradition, sentiment and, some would say, common sense. It was in a lunch queue at Oxford that he was converted to vegetarianism. He soon took up the cause of animal rights and in 1975 published *Animal Liberation* – a work that sold over 500,000 copies and provided the intellectual force for an entire movement. It was in this and other books that he set out his most ambitious expansion of our ethical life – the multiplication of morally relevant individuals to include non-human animals.

In 2003, the South African novelist J. M. Coetzee wrote in *Elizabeth Costello* that due to the slaughter of animals for food on an industrial scale 'we are surrounded by an enterprise of degradation, cruelty and killing which rivals anything that the Third Reich was capable of'. Unlike the ordinary German people who went about their daily lives while the Nazis rounded up the Jews from their neighbourhoods, carnivores are actively participating in the mass murder of the present day. According to Singer, our descendants may one day look upon us as savages for this 'crime of stupefying proportions'. Professor Singer is associated with the animal rights movement, although, as a utilitarian, he does not believe in rights as such. What matters is that things work out for the best, and rights are valid only insofar as they promote that end. Nevertheless, the prospect of rights for animals has been with utilitarianism since its birth. In the eighteenth century, Jeremy Bentham, the founder of utilitarianism, wrote of the wickedness of deeming the colour of someone's skin to be justification for enslaving them, adding:

> The day may come, when the rest of the animal creation may acquire those rights which never could have been withholden from them but by the hand of tyranny ... It may come one day to be recognized, that the number of legs, the villosity of the skin, or the termination of the *os sacrum*, are reasons equally insufficient for abandoning a sensitive being to the same fate. What else is it that should trace the insuperable line? Is it the faculty of reason, or perhaps, the faculty for discourse?[2]

The answer is no, for 'a full-grown horse or dog is beyond comparison a more rational, as well as a more conversable animal, than an infant'. The important question, Bentham decides, is 'not, Can they *reason*? nor, Can they *talk*? but, Can they *suffer*?' Few would deny that at least the higher animals can feel the sensation of pain as humans do, and if they did not then there would be no point in cosmetics researchers testing their products by applying them to the eyes of rabbits.

I asked Singer if it made any difference that the animals slaughtered for food would never have lived had they not been bred for that purpose. He replied. 'I think it would be better for factory farmed animals if they did not exist. Their lives do not contain any positive qualities.' But some animals live far better, longer lives on farms than they would in the wild, where they might lack regular access to food, warmth and shelter. Even their slaughter under humane conditions might be less unpleasant than a slow death from disease or the agony of being devoured alive by a predator. Singer is relaxed about these objections, though also eager to stress that most meat production is not humane. He does not condemn those he calls 'conscientious carnivores', who consume only those animals who have led lives of natural bliss on organic farms. When I remarked that his sweater looked like it was made of wool, he looked down at its cuffs and shrugged, 'It might be. Look, I'm not a fanatic. I wouldn't go out and buy wool, but there's no point in throwing out what I've been given over the years. Because I'm a consequentialist I think about where it is going to make a difference.'

It is difficult to criticize the position of a utilitarian rationalist, for if you should point out a way in which their thesis leads to an unwelcome result, they simply modify the thesis – for their position is defined as whatever leads to the best result. Singer is not insensitive to the important differences between humans and other animals – one of which is our greater ability to anticipate our suffering:

Suppose we decided to perform lethal scientific experiments on normal adult humans, kidnapped at random from public parks for this purpose. Soon, every adult who entered the park would become fearful of being kidnapped for experimentation. The resultant terror would be a form of suffering additional to whatever pain was involved in the experiment itself. The same experiments carried out on non-human animals would cause less suffering overall, for the non-human animals would not have the same anticipatory dread. This does not mean, I hasten to add, that it is all right to experiment with animals as we please; but only that if the experiment *is* to be done at all, there is *some* reason, compatible with the equal consideration of interests, for preferring to use non-human animals rather than normal adult humans.[3]

It is not that Singer loves animals or hates people. He writes:

The assumption that in order to be interested in such matters one must be an 'animal lover' is itself an indication of the absence of the slightest inkling that the moral standards that we apply among human beings might extend to other animals. No one, except a racist concerned to smear his opponents as 'nigger lovers', would suggest that in order to be concerned about equality for mistreated racial minorities you have to love those minorities, or regard them as cute and cuddly. So why make this assumption about people who work for improvements in the conditions of animals?[4]

Singer demands that we practise the Socratic virtue of consistency. So, if medical researchers wish to experiment on live animals, they must also consider practising on brain-damaged humans with equivalent faculties. In Singer's ethical calculus, what matter are preferences, interests and the ability to suffer, and humans are not the only creatures to possess all three. On the other hand, some humans – such as those in a persistent vegetative state – lack the requisite traits for personhood, and we need treat such unfortunates no better than the unenlightened presently treat beasts. Whatever rights we give to humans, we cannot deny them to animals just because they are not human (though there may be other reasons). The idea of animal rights is sometimes casually dismissed on the grounds that rights imply duties. Indeed they do, but there is no implication that the recipient of the right and the holder of the concomitant duty must be one and the same individual. We accord rights to infants even though we do not expect them to fulfil their end of any 'bargain'.

For Singer, the privileges of animals even include the right to have sexual intercourse with their owners. The professor wrote a notorious defence of bestiality in a review of the book *Dearest Pet*. When I asked if he had been serious, he responded as if there was nothing remarkable about the thought: 'A dog can lick a woman's genitals if it wants, or it can walk away. There's nothing wrong with that if there's no coercion involved.' It would be easy to criticize here – what about a young puppy that didn't know what it was doing, was induced by dog biscuits or told that it could play with some boys and girls? However, Professor Singer's point is that we, too, are part of the animal kingdom, and that our ethics should reflect that realization.

Singer hopes for a 'Copernican Revolution' in ethics that takes account of Darwin's ideas – a new moral universe in which human life is no longer at the centre. But even if God is taken out of the moral picture, it is far from clear that there would be a demand for universalism, the view that one can recognize no 'special interests', such as attachments to family and friends over strangers, in an ethical decision. The problem that most philosophers have with Singer is his refusal to provide a foundation for his strident views. When I talked to Sir Bernard Williams about Peter Singer, he described the Australian's ideas as 'a ghastly form of quasi-religious dogmatism'. The man he referred to as 'the dreaded Singer' isn't 'even interested in the foundations of the principle of utility. The question of why we should think that our entire lives are guided by one simple principle gets swept away in a few pages, and then we get on to explaining with great enthusiasm how, if we adopt this principle, then almost everything we do is wrong.'

Singer's reluctance to concentrate on first principles is understandable given his view of what morality consists in. According to his 'Preference Utilitarianism', the morally right thing to do is that which satisfies the preferences of the greatest number of people (as opposed to Jeremy Bentham's 'Hedonistic Utilitarianism', under which the utilitarian goal is the maximization of pleasure for the greatest number). However, if indeed there is no more to morality than satisfying people's preferences, it adds nothing to say that such conduct is 'morally correct'. So the force of the utilitarian principle cannot come from the realization that it is the 'moral truth', but from our existing agreement that this principle is always morally right. In a sense Singer is not trying to convince us of anything, but rather attempting to work within what he thinks we already, latently, believe. Since there is no transcendent source of goodness in Singer's utilitarian ethics, right is a matter of following through on our rational judgements, which are based upon premisses. Although he is a fierce critic of the idea of following our instincts, these premisses are themselves instincts of a kind, even if they are located in the head rather than the heart. Once the principle of utility is spelled out, it seems we are supposed to think that this is what we have been trying to articulate through our actions all along. Unfortunately for Singer, this is not the universal reaction to his efforts.

Philosophical arguments for utilitarian principles are necessary, because some of the consequences of Singer's ideas will strike most of us as absurd and unrealistic. If we had the option of saving either a four-year-old girl or a family of cats from a burning building we would not hesitate to rescue the girl. This is a brute instinctual preference, and whether we should maintain it depends on what we identify as the purpose of ethics – to put prejudices in coherent order or to decide what beliefs we should have. Consideration for animals is one thing, but granting them equal status with humans is another. There are some individuals to whom we have a special moral relation, such as our friends, family and those we have taken into our care. When Singer hears such objections he notes their similarity to a remark made by Reichsmarshal Hermann Göring: 'I think with my blood.' It was gut instinct that built the death camps, not rationality as is often supposed by those who distrust the Enlightenment.

Singer does not believe that anyone should have a special weight in terms of preferential treatment within the utilitarian calculations – not even the person doing the calculating. However, he has his work cut out if he wishes to extend his care to everything that suffers. The English philosopher Roger Scruton writes that:

> Abstracting from my interest does not mean consulting yours. It is
> the duty of a judge to set aside his own interests in order to do
> justice. But this does not mean that he arrives at the just solution by

considering the interests of anybody else, still less the interests of everyone – otherwise, he would never arrive at a judgment.[5]

We need to cut out many individuals' interests if we are not to become bogged down in the simplest ethical decision – for we can never predict all the consequences of all of our actions. Immanuel Kant's principle that 'where there is no can there is no ought' would seem to absolve us of any wrongdoing here but, as Scruton would point out, Kant was not a utilitarian like Professor Singer. Singer's world is one of moral hopelessness, where we seem doomed to do wrong, though we are obliged to attempt the impossible task of doing right. The professor assured me that that there is no paradox, and that we need only do our best, because: 'We cannot be blamed if, for reasons impossible to foresee, our attempts to do what will have the best consequences go astray.' But it is precisely the foreseeable, and unmanageable, that Scruton has in mind.

Singer's attempt to navigate the moral maze presented by utilitarianism has led him to make enemies more dangerous than Roger Scruton. Although we cannot predict the future, we can at least, he believes, be clear about the present. He writes that: 'There is no rule that says that a potential x has the same values as an x or has all the rights of an x. There are many examples that show just the contrary. To pull out a sprouting acorn is not the same as cutting down a venerable oak.'[6] If we are untroubled by boiling an egg where we would not dream of doing the same to a live adult chicken, this should tell us something about the so-called 'right to life' of the unborn fetus. Indeed, one could say that Professor Singer, in famously infanticidal moments, has considered abortion to be permissible several weeks *after* birth should the child be severely disabled. For these views Singer has received more than the bile of rival thinkers. His appointment to a Professorship at Princeton in 1999 led to several days of angry protest outside the faculty, and wealthy business tycoon Steve Forbes vowed not to donate any more money to the college. During a lecture on disabled children in Germany in 1989, he was shouted down by his audience, one of whom took to the stage and smashed his glasses. There, as on many other occasions, he was accused of Nazi sympathies, even though his parents were Austrian Jewish refugees and three of his grandparents died in concentration camps. He protests that he has nothing against the disabled, but points out that by bringing up such a child, a couple with limited resources are, as it were, depriving a future, healthy child of a far more fulfilled life. It may seem strange to consider individuals who do not actually exist yet, but as a utilitarian he is at least being consistent in desiring a world with as many satisfied preferences as possible.

For a would-be fascist, Singer locates himself very much on the political left. Although he has little sympathy for certain core beliefs of the left, such as collective ownership, he favours systematic charity towards one's fellow humans. He urges American households to give away 70 per cent of their income to the poor and spends little on luxuries himself. The fount of social problems, he argues, is that human morality grew out of the natural principles of tit-for-tat and mutual backscratching. If the poor become so weak that nothing they do can affect the wealthy, any incentive for cooperation will break down – threatening to take society with it:

> If nothing you do really makes much difference to me, tit for tat
> will not work. So while equality is not required, too great a
> disparity in power or wealth will remove the incentive for mutual

cooperation. If you leave a group of people so far outside the social commonwealth that they have nothing to contribute to it, you alienate them from the social practices and institutions of which they are part; and they almost certainly become adversaries who pose a threat to those institutions.[7]

In a sense he is not asking for anything new, merely appealing to our rationality – for distance does strange things to our moral sense. According to the '3,000-mile rule', some individuals believe that there is nothing wrong with committing adultery if they are away from home – as if this is somehow better than conducting an affair with one's next-door neighbour. The same thinking means that we can sit unmoved by the knowledge that someone on the other side of the world does not have enough food to eat, even though we would never allow someone to starve to death on our own doorstep. Yet, by declining to send money to the poor overseas, we are condemning them no less than we would those nearer to home if we abolished the welfare system. These are natural reactions common to almost all of us even though the infrastructure of the modern world enables us to extend our charity around the globe if we wish. Yet we would never assert that the number of miles between ourselves and someone who needs our help should be a moral consideration. To act as if it does betrays 'distancism'.

Singer's brand of utilitarianism constitutes a paternalistic leftism. It acknowledges only the preferences that people would have in ideal conditions. So a peasant woman's preference to remain chained to her kitchen stove is to be discounted in favour of the contrary preference she would have if she had had access to a Western education. The utilitarian abacus is to be operated by those in the know, who are aware of people's 'best interests' and are prepared to act on them, even though the beneficiaries of their goodwill might not be. In Singer's society, this would not be achieved by riding roughshod over the preferences of the 'ignorant', but would involve gently coaxing them to the point where they realize the need for change. Hopefully, they will not be like a good part of the world's population and be too stubborn to see sense soon enough.

Singer is confident that such prospects are good, for he appears to have history on his side. In looking forward to a day when the prejudice of what he calls 'speciesism' will go the way of sexism, classism and homophobia, he is imagining the obvious next step in a historical process: the famous 'expanding circle' of the historian W. H. Lecky that has brought moral parity to an ever greater variety of agents. The supposed endorsement of history has perhaps given Singer a shield against the personal abuse to which he has been subjected. It has also given a serenity to his arguments – there is none of the self-righteous hectoring that typifies so many of those with whom he agrees in the animal rights lobby. However, he does not seem to consider that the expanding circle may have a dark interior. The process can be seen as a positive development or it can be viewed cynically as a levelling down, wherein peoples and species end up as equally worthless. It depends whether animals acquire the value of humans or humans are reduced to the status of animals. Values derived from human whim will be held less inviolate than when they were taken to represent the will of God expressed via our consciences.

As our sphere of concern has become broader we have begun to witness the phenomenon of 'moral thinning'. The philosopher Friedrich Nietzsche once suggested that the roots of moral observance lay in legal concerns, that it was originally a kind of living repayment to creditors who had died. We can hardly be surprised if today morality is returning from whence it came and collapsing into a mere concern for the laws of the land. This process is well under way in the West if the recent history of the insurance industry is indicative. Personal injury claimants feel no shame if the letter of the law enables them to extract huge punitive damages from companies that could not reasonably have prevented their injury. Moral dilemmas are 'settled' by recourse to the United States Constitution every time a sick, elderly relative is abandoned in a state retirement home by a family who does not wish to look after them. Politicians guilty of heinous moral failures routinely defend their right to continue in their posts on the grounds that they 'did nothing illegal'. In nations obsessed by law, it is perhaps to be expected that where one has not broken any laws one is thought to have done no wrong. Singer's 'Copernican Revolution' may not lead to the enlightenment he imagines. In the short term, however, things seem to be on course. I once asked the prominent American moral philosopher Christine Korsgaard whether she believed that studying ethics made those in her profession better people. 'Well,' she replied after thinking for a moment, 'most of us are vegetarians.'

the meaning of life and death

A quick test of the assertion that enjoyment outweighs pain in this world, or that they are at any rate balanced, would be to compare the feelings of an animal engaged in eating another with those of the animal being eaten.

Arthur Schopenhauer

A man goes to India, consults a sage in a cave and asks him the meaning of life. In three sentences the sage tells him, the man thanks him and leaves. There are several variants of this story also: In the first, the man lives meaningfully ever after; in the second he makes the sentences public so that everyone then knows the meaning of life; in the third, he sets the sentences to rock music, making his fortune and enabling everyone to whistle the meaning of life; and in the fourth variant, his plane crashes as he is flying off from his meeting with the sage. In the fifth version, the person listening to me tell this story eagerly asks what sentences the sage spoke... And in the sixth version, I tell him.

A parody by Robert Nozick

Before his death in 2002, the Oxford philosopher R. M. Hare liked to tell the story of how a Swiss teenager staying in his house suddenly changed from his normal sunny disposition to one of morbid depression. Hare was moved to act after the boy ceased to eat his meals, took to wandering the countryside after dark and most tellingly, 'surprised us one morning by asking for cigarettes – he had not smoked at all up until then'. The influence of French philosophy was unmistakable and, sure enough, it transpired that the young houseguest had suffered a psychological shock one evening after reading *The Outsider* by the existentialist Albert Camus. Like Mersault, the hero of the great novel, he had concluded that 'nothing matters'. The cure was simple. Hare wrote:

> My friend had not understood that the function of the word 'matters' is to express concern; he had thought that mattering was something (some activity or process) that things did, rather like chattering; as if the sentence 'My wife matters to me' were similar in logical function to the sentence 'My wife chatters to me'. If one thinks that, one may begin to wonder what this activity is, called mattering; and one may begin to observe the world closely (aided perhaps by the clear cold descriptions of a novel like that of Camus) to see if one can catch anything doing something that can be called mattering; and when we can observe nothing going on which seems to correspond to this name, it is easy for the novelist to persuade us that after all *nothing matters*. To which the answer is, '"Matters" isn't that sort of word; it isn't intended to *describe* something that things do, but to express our concern about what they do; so of course we can't observe things *mattering*; but that doesn't mean that they don't matter … My Swiss friend was not a hypocrite. His trouble was that, through philosophical naiveté, he took for a real moral problem what was not a moral problem at all, but a philosophical one – a problem to be solved, not by an

agonising struggle with his soul, but by an attempt to understand what he was saying.'[1]

Hare's houseguest might have been cured by another masterpiece by Camus, *The Myth of Sisyphus*. Sisyphus was the man who offended the gods by refusing to accept his death. He was condemned to push a boulder to the top of a hill, from where it would roll down to the bottom again. There the process would begin anew, and continue forever. Camus concludes:

> It is during that return, that pause, that Sisyphus interests me. A face that toils so close to stones is already stone itself! I see that man going back down with a heavy yet measured step towards the torment of which he will never know the end. That hour like a breathing-space which returns as surely as his suffering, that is the hour of consciousness. At each of those moments when he leaves the heights and gradually sinks towards the lairs of the gods, he is superior to his fate. He is stronger than rock … The lucidity that was to constitute his torture at the same time crowns his victory. There is no fate that cannot be surmounted by scorn.[2]

The American philosopher Richard Taylor framed the terms of the debate on the meaning of life in the world of English-speaking analytic philosophy. Taylor served as a submarine officer during the Second World War, but ended his life a pacifist. He is remembered as an epicure, an authority on bee-keeping, a writer of books on love and relationships and a certified marriage guidance counsellor who had been married three times himself. He liked to smoke cigars while giving classes and, though he switched to flasks of tea in his later years, he died of lung cancer at the age of eighty-three in 2003. Taylor concurred with Camus that Sisyphus can find solace, but identified two opposing approaches to the problem. The first is from the outside – if, for example, 'we supposed that these stones … were assembled at the top of the hill … in a beautiful and enduring temple'.[3]

To look at the issue 'from the outside' is to identify objective sources of meaning in the world that we might hope to cleave to. These are the sort of values that the Swiss boy apparently failed to find on his long walks. Traditionally, they came from a heavenly Creator, the 'demise' of whom led to the existentialists' worries. However, if the question is asked, 'How can life have meaning without God?', the next question should be, 'How exactly does life have meaning *with* God?' The point is that God's purpose must itself be a meaningful one, and it recalls the ancient conundrum of whether good things are good because the gods love them, or whether the gods love them because they are good. If God could have decreed that evil acts were good and vice versa, then to act virtuously in order to please Him is no more than to obey divine whim. Similarly, any purpose of human existence that the Deity has in mind must be meaningful regardless of His wishes. (Needless to say, the same also follows for the intentions of one's mortal parents.) If it is worth living well in the sight of God, it is worth living well without it. It may be in our interests to follow the divine plan – so as not to go to hell perhaps – but in that case we are subject to duress. Whether this situation truly represents the meaning of my life may come down to my word versus His. Any meaning given from without is one that we can take or leave, though this is not to deny, of course, that some people will accept happily a purpose that has been imposed upon them. The same goes for the one-word answer to the meaning of life given by Darwinism: reproduction. Procreation is certainly in the 'interests' of our genes, because that is what they are geared to achieve, but many individuals feel that their own interests as idiosyncratic human beings are quite different and treat their biological imperative with the scorn Camus's Sisyphus reserves for the gods.

In the end, as the Oxford philosopher David Wiggins writes:

'Unless we are Marxists, we are much more resistant in the second half of the twentieth century than eighteenth or nineteenth century men knew how to be against attempts to locate the meaning of human life or human history in mystical or metaphysical conceptions – in the emancipation of mankind, or progress, or the onward advance of Absolute Spirit. It is not that we have lost interest in emancipation or progress themselves. But, whether temporarily or permanently, we have more or less abandoned the idea that the importance of emancipation or progress ... is that these are marks by which our minute speck in the universe can distinguish itself as the spiritual focus of the cosmos.[4]

But if we are orphans to meaning, this does nothing to devalue any purpose we find or create for ourselves. Many couples find it very difficult to conceive and spend a great deal of time and money on fertility treatments in order to fulfil their desire for a family. Yet is the life of a baby born to such parents more meaningful than that of a child conceived by two strangers during a drunken encounter? We know it would be offensive and absurd to suggest so. One cannot inherit meaningfulness any more than one can truly inherit nobility or the right to rule. The embryo in the IVF tube might grow up to be a delinquent, while the child of the broom cupboard might become the lynchpin of its family and a pillar of the community.

We seem to be left with Richard Taylor's second approach: the attempt to find meaning internally, from within oneself. The problem with Sisyphus building a temple on top of the hill is that monuments do not last forever, and even those that do (like the pyramids, Taylor adds) soon become curiosities. One also has to wonder how long it is going to take Sisyphus to complete his temple: either he will finish it and then be condemned to boredom thereafter, or else it will never be finished, which makes the exercise rather pointless. But, Taylor writes:

> Suppose that the gods, as an afterthought, waxed perversely merciful by implanting in [Sisyphus] a strange and irrational impulse … to roll stones … To make this more graphic, suppose they accomplish this by implanting in him some substance that has this effect on his character and drives … this little afterthought of the gods … was … merciful. For they have by this device managed to give Sisyphus precisely what he wants – by making him want precisely what they inflict on him. However it may appear to us, Sisyphus' … life is now filled with mission and meaning, and he seems to himself to have been given an entry to heaven … The *only* thing that has happened is this: Sisyphus has been reconciled to [his existence] … He has been led to embrace it. Not, however, by reason or persuasion, but by nothing more rational than the potency of a new substance in his veins … The meaning of life is from within us, it is not bestowed from without, and it far exceeds in its beauty and permanence any heaven of which men have ever dreamed or yearned for.[5]

This kind of hyperbole is more often heard from the mouths of lesser thinkers than Taylor – namely, mystics and gurus. The same point is expressed by the modern adage that 'If you can't have what you like, then you'd better like what you have' and prompts the obvious concern that what you have may not be worth liking. As David Wiggins puts it, in Taylor's scenario:

> It seems to make too little difference to the meaningfulness of life how well or badly our strivings are apt to turn out. Stone rolling for its own sake, and stone rolling for successful temple building, and stone rolling for temple building that will be frustrated – all seem to come to much the same thing.[6]

As human beings we want not only to satisfy our desires, but also for those desires to be legitimate, or the best ones we could have. We want our achievements to mean something objectively, or at least compared to those of others, and not just as a way of proving something to ourselves. Nor would it make a difference if the substance put in Sisyphus's veins had been flowing through them since birth rather than injected at a later date; the 'mercy' of the gods is no less deceitful for having a longer history. Just as any divine purpose would have to be meaningful regardless of God's approval, so must the designs of individual mortals.

The Australian philosopher Peter Singer complains:

> Until my arrival in New York, I had never met anyone who was seeing a psychotherapist as much as once a week; but as I became acquainted with a circle of New York Professors and their spouses, I soon found that many of them were in daily psychoanalysis. Five

days a week, eleven months of the year, they had an appointment
for one hour, not to be broken under any circumstances short of a
life or death emergency. They could not go on holiday unless their
analyst was taking a holiday at the same time...Some of my
colleagues, well-paid, successful academics, were handing over a
quarter of their annual salary to their analysts! This was for people
who, as far as I could tell, were neither more nor less disturbed
than those not in analysis...I wanted to pick them up and shake
them... In looking inwards for solutions to their problems, people
are seeking the mysterious substance that, in Taylor's second
possible way of adding meaning to the life of Sisyphus, the gods
put into Sisyphus in order to make him want to push stones up
the hill.[7]

Singer strongly favours the temple option:

If these able, affluent New Yorkers had only got off their analysts'
couches, stopped thinking about their own problems, and gone out
to do something about the real problems faced by less fortunate
people in Bangladesh and Ethiopia – or even in Manhattan, a few
subway stops north – they would have forgotten their own
problems and maybe made the world a better place as well.[8]

The analysts of New York seem to have traded in a doctrine
beloved of talk show hosts and Eastern gurus: that happiness and a
meaningful life can be attained by simply altering one's attitudes. The
serum of Sisyphus has taken over from the elixir of youth as the
exemplary target of a hopeless search. The unhappy are told that they
must change their outlook when what they really need is to change

their life – get a divorce or a new career or ensure that their child's drug addiction is dealt with.

A student once asked the English linguistic philosopher J. L. Austin to explain what 'existing' was. Austin replied that it was 'like breathing, only quieter'. It is not surprising that the naked background of life, divested of any meaning-giving activities, should often be thought rather purposeless. We might wonder how such a featureless vessel possibly *could* have a purpose. The very notion of purposes breaks down if we widen its scope too far. The purpose, meaning or value of any object is a relation it has to something outside itself. For example, the value of a hammer is the use to which a carpenter puts it, the value of a child is the emotional attachment felt by its mother, the purpose of antibiotics is to kill harmful bacteria. When we come to assess the value of an individual's entire life, we must likewise look for something outside it – to his or her impact on history, perhaps, or to the family they nurture. Again, being something external to an individual's life, it need not be something that he or she necessarily cares for. Many dogs are bought for the purpose of guarding property, but this does not stop some of them from greeting burglars by wagging their tails.

The problem of an individual life threatens to re-emerge in a wider theatre – the meaning of all things. If the context in which our lives have meaning itself has no meaning, then the canker of meaninglessness might spread all the way down. As the American moral philosopher Kurt Baier complains: 'People are disconcerted by the thought that *life as such* has no meaning in that sense only because they very naturally think it entails that no individual life can have meaning either. They naturally assume that *this* life or *that* life can have meaning only if *life as such* has meaning.'[9] John Wisdom,

Wittgenstein's successor as Professor of Philosophy at Cambridge, was sympathetic. He wrote that:

> Whenever we ask, 'What supports thing A or these things A, B, C,' then we can answer this question by mentioning some thing other than the thing A or things A, B, C about which we asked 'What supports it or them?' We must if we are to answer the question mention something D other than those things which form the subject of our question, and we must say that this thing is what supports them. If we mean by the phrase 'all things' absolutely all things which exist then obviously there is nothing outside that about which we are now asked 'What supports all this?' Consequently, any answer to the question will be self-contradictory just as any answer to the question 'What is bigger than the biggest of all things' must be self-contradictory. Such questions are absurd, or, if you like, silly and senseless ... Perhaps someone here replies, the meaning, the significance of this present life, lies in a life hereafter, a life in heaven. All right. But imagine that some persistent enquirer asks, 'But what I am asking is what is the meaning of all life, life here and life beyond, life now and life hereafter? What is the meaning of all things in earth and heaven?' Are we to say that this question is absurd because there cannot be anything beyond all things while at the same time any answer to 'What is the meaning of all things?' must point to some thing beyond all things?[10]

Wisdom answers that the question is not entirely senseless. Rather:

we are trying to find the order in the drama of Time ... We must however remember that what one calls answering such a question is not giving an answer. I mean we cannot answer such a question in the form: 'The meaning is this.' Such an idea about what form answering a question must take may lead to a new despair in which we feel we cannot do anything in the way of answering such a question as 'What is the meaning in it all?' merely because we are not able to sum up our results in a phrase or formula.[11]

Camus observed that 'What is called a reason for living is also an excellent reason for dying.'[12] But a meaningful life and a meaningful death are not the same thing. History records innumerable no-hopers who met their end by saving another's life, while Elvis Presley died on the lavatory. The meaning of death nonetheless has a myth-ical bearing on the meaning of life. In the first century BC, Lucretius wrote in *On the Nature of Things*:

Look back at the eternity that passed before we were born, and mark how utterly it counts to us as nothing. This is a mirror that Nature holds up to us, in which we may see the time that shall be after we are dead. Is there anything terrifying in the sight – anything depressing – anything that is not more restful than the soundest sleep?

Derek Parfit concludes:

If we are afraid of death ... the object of our dread is not our *non-existence*. It is only our *future* non-existence. That we can think serenely of our past non-existence does not show that it is not something to regret. But since we do not in fact view with dread our past non-existence, we may be able to use this fact to reduce our dread, or depression, when we think about our inevitable deaths. If we often think about, and view serenely, the blackness behind us, some of this serenity may be transferred to our view of the blackness before us.[13]

The Austrian psychiatrist Victor Frankl argued that dread has its place, as it is death that gives life its meaning – on the grounds that the prospect of certain doom works wonders for self-discipline. 'If we were immortal,' he wrote, 'we could legitimately postpone every action forever. It would be of no consequence whether or not we did a thing now; every act might just as well be done tomorrow or the day after or a year from now or ten years hence.'[14] In contrast to this eternal Mexico, we must instead take our earthly opportunities while we can. But it is not as though we can miss opportunities when we are dead, as there will be no 'us' to miss anything. The advice would be valid for someone looking to pack as much activity as possible into a two-week vacation, but it cannot apply to an entire lifetime in quite the same way. Besides, death makes us question whether it is worth bothering to do anything while we are here, given that one day no trace will remain of our accomplishments.

This last thought partakes in the obsession with size that bedevils the debate. Science shows us that human beings on Planet Earth are, on the one hand, a speck of dust on a speck of dust – barely notice-able on the cosmic scale – but also shows effectively that the smaller something is the closer to true reality it comes, for macroscopic events and objects are no more than the effects of the microscopic processes of microscopic particles. This is the level upon which the fundamental laws of nature operate. Although medium-sized objects such as ourselves may seem to have been left out somewhere in the chain of being, it should not be assumed that physicists have therefore rendered us irrelevant, or ever intended such a thing. Irrelevant to what, we might ask. Thomas Nagel reminds us that: 'It is often remarked that nothing we do now will matter in a million years. But if that is true, then by the same token, nothing that will be the case in a million years matters now.'[15]

Our meagre bodies may limit the scope of our physical undertakings, but this is different from undermining their significance. Olympic gold medals for sprinting are not devalued because cheetahs and horses can run even faster. Neither, in the same way, does the finite duration of our lives reduce their significance. The American philosopher Robert Nozick ridiculed the idea that it should: 'Consider those things people speak of as permanent and eternal. These include (apart from God) numbers, sets, abstract ideas, spacetime itself. Would it be better to be one of these things? ... Is anyone pining to lead a setly existence?'[16] Even if we could do this, this would not make our lives more meaningful. We are each of us out-existed by rocks, oak trees and giant tortoises, yet only extreme environmentalists deem such objects to be more important than the human race. As Ludwig Wittgenstein mused:

> Not only is there no guarantee of the temporal immortality of the human soul, that is to say of its eternal survival after death; but, in any case, this assumption completely fails to accomplish the purpose for which it has always been intended. Or is some riddle solved by my surviving forever? Is not this eternal life itself as much of a riddle as our present life?[17]

A. W. Moore writes:

> I might be appalled at the thought that I shall live forever, without, at any particular time in the future, wanting *these* to be my last five minutes. (That is, I might never want to die without wanting never to die.) More starkly, I might be appalled at the thought that I shall live forever *and* appalled at the thought that I shall one day die ... There is no reason why either option should attract me – though there is no third alternative.[18]

The second option is the one that occupies us most. As Thomas Nagel averred: 'Given the simple choice between living for another week and dying in five minutes I would always choose to live for another week ... I conclude that I would be glad to live forever.'[19] Wittgenstein remarked that: 'Death is not an event in life: we do not live to experience death.'[20] And, as Moore puts it, 'My death never *comes for me.*' However, Wittgenstein added that: 'If we take eternity to mean not temporal duration but timelessness, then eternal life belongs to those who live in the present. Our life has no end in just the way in which our visual field has no limits.'

Unfortunately, most of us do indeed take eternity to mean temporal duration, which is why we spend so much time worrying about eternal life. And while our life may not have limits that we experience just as our field of vision does not have borders that we can see on both sides of, this no more means that we possess life eternal than its corollary means that we can see all things on Earth. Unlike the problem of life, the problem of death admits of no dissolution. Our fear of non-existence is a set-up on the part of Nature. There would be no point in a creature fearing something that it could not hope to change, such as the time of its birth. However, there is a great deal of point in being afraid of one's death, because one has some degree of control over the timing. Instinct is a blunt instrument. It continues to hope, and continues to make us cower, even where death is inevitable.

notes

Preface

1 *The Best Mind Since Einstein* (NOVA US VHS, originally broadcast on PBS TV, 1993).

Chapter 1

1 Thomas Reid, *Essays on the Intellectual Powers of Man*, ed. A. D. Woozley (London: Macmillan and Co., 1941), p. 203.

2 'The Self and the Future', in *Philosophical Review* 79(2) (April 1970): 161–80.

3 Ray Kurzweil, *The Age of Spiritual Machines* (London: Orion Business Books, 1999), p. 129.

4 *Reasons and Persons*, 3rd edn (Oxford: Oxford University Press, 1987), p. 256.

5 Ibid., p. 277.

6 Ibid., p. 281.

7 Ibid.

Chapter 2

1 Quoted in Victor Grassian, *Moral Reasoning* (New Jersey: Prentice Hall, 1992), p. 166.

2 *A Philosophical Essay on Probabilities*, The World of Mathematics, vol. 2, ed. James R.

Newman (Redmond: Tempus, 1988), pp. 1301–02.

3 *On the Genealogy of Morals*, I, 13, in *Basic Writings of Nietzsche*, trans. and ed. Walter Kaufmann (New York: The Modern Library, 1992), p. 481.

4 *An Essay Concerning Human Understanding*, Bk II, ch. XI, section X (London: Everyman, 1993), p. 125.

5 See 'The Neural Time Factor in Conscious and Unconscious Events', in *Experimental and Theoretical Studies of Consciousness*, Ciba Foundation Symposium 174 (London: John Wiley and Sons, 1993), pp. 123–37.

6 *Mortal Questions* (New York: Cambridge University Press, 1979), p. 37.

7 Ibid.

8 'Responsibility and Control', in Fischer (ed.), *Moral Responsibility* (Ithaca, NY: Cornell University Press, 1986), pp. 174–90; example is introduced on p. 176.

9 *Elbow Room* (Cambridge, Mass.: MIT Press, 1984), p. 8.

10 Ibid., p. 72 (my italics).

11 *Philosophical Explanations*
(Oxford: Clarendon Press, 1981),
p. 315.

Chapter 3

1 *Minds, Brains and Science*
(Harmondsworth: Penguin,
1984), p. 44.
2 *De Anima*, 'On The Soul', Book
II, *The Complete Works of
Aristotle Volume One*, ed.
Jonathan Barnes (Princeton:
Princeton University Press,
1984), p. 657.
3 A. M. Turing, 'Computing
Machinery and Intelligence',
Mind LIX: 433–60.
4 See Hans Moravec, 'When Will
Computer Hardware Match the
Human Brain?', *Journal of
Evolution and Technology 1*
(1998), available online at:
<http://www.
transhumanist.com/volume1/
moravec.htm>.
5 See Nick Bostrom, 'When
Machines Outsmart Humans',
Futures 35(7): 759–64.
6 'Minds, Brains, and Programs',
Behavioral and Brain Sciences 3
(1980): 417–24.
7 At the Rochester Conference,
documented in M. M. Lucas and
P. J. Hayes (eds), *Proceedings of
the Cognitive Curriculum
Conference* (New York:
University of Rochester, 1982).

8 *On The Contrary: Critical Essays,
1987–1997* (Cambridge, Mass.:
MIT Press, 1998), p. 53.
9 Daniel C. Dennett, *Darwin's
Dangerous Idea*
(Harmondsworth: Penguin,
1996), p. 399.
10 Daniel C. Dennett,
Consciousness Explained
(Harmondsworth: Penguin,
1993), p. 269.
11 *Are We Spiritual Machines?: Ray
Kurzweil vs the Critics of Strong
AI* (Seattle: The Discovery
Institute, 2002), p. 64.

Chapter 4

1 'Discourse on Method', Pt IV, in
*Discourse on Method and the
Meditations*, trans. F. E. Sutcliffe
(London: Penguin, 1968), p. 54.
2 'The Zombie Within', *Nature* 411
(21 June 2001).
3 'What Mary Didn't Know',
Journal of Philosophy 83 (1986):
291–5.

Chapter 5

1 'Are You Living in a Computer
Simulation?', *Philosophical
Quarterly* 53(211) (2003): 243–55;
available online at:
<http://www.simulation-
argument.com/simulation.
htm>.
2 Ibid.
3 'How to Live in a Simulation',

Journal of Evolution and Technology 7 (September 2001); available online at <http://www.transhumanist.com/volume7/simulation.html>.

4 Ibid.

5 *Critique of Pure Reason*, Preface to 2nd edn, trans. Norman Kemp-Smith, p. 34.

6 Such instances are known as 'Gettier cases' after the American philosopher Edmund Gettier, who first constructed them in a 1963 paper comprising just over 900 words and three footnotes: 'Is Knowledge Justified True Belief?' in *Analysis* 26 (1963): 144–6.

7 'A Causal Theory of Knowledge', *Journal of Philosophy* 64 (1967): 357–72.

8 'The Need to Know', in Marjorie Clay and Keith Lehrer (eds), *Knowledge and Skepticism* (Boulder, CO: Westview Press, 1989): p. 95.

9 The example is from Gilbert Harman's *Thought* (Princeton: Princeton University Press, 1973), pp. 143–4.

10 *Warrant and Proper Function* (Oxford: Oxford University Press, 1993), p. 225.

Chapter 6

1 'Meaning and Reference', *Journal of Philosophy* (1973): 699–711.

2 An account of Putnam Sr is contained in Bertram D. Wolfe, *Strange Communists I Have Known* (New York: Stein & Day, 1965), pp. 72–80.

3 See 'The Meaning of "Meaning"', in *Philosophical Papers, Vol. II: Mind, Language, and Reality* (Cambridge: Cambridge University Press, 1975), pp. 215–71.

4 'Individualism and the Mental', *Midwestern Studies in Philosophy* 4 (1979): 73–122.

5 *Words and Life*, 3rd edn (Cambridge, Mass.: Harvard University Press, 1996), pp. 443–4.

6 'Knowing One's Own Mind', *Proceedings of the Aristotelian Society* 60 (1987): 441–58.

7 *Language, Thought and Other Biological Categories* (Cambridge, Mass. and London: MIT Press, 1984), p. 93.

8 'Cutting Philosophy of Language Down to Size', in Anthony O'Hear (ed.), *Philosophy at the New Millennium* (Cambridge: Cambridge University Press, 2001), p. 134.

9 'The Wisdom of Repugnance', *The New Republic*, 2 June 1997.

Chapter 7

1 *Armies of the Night* (Harmondsworth: Penguin

1968), pp. 191–2.

2 *The Hague*: Mouton & Co., 1957.

3 'The Role of Language in Intelligence', in Jean Khalfa (ed.), *What is Intelligence? The Darwin College Lectures* (Cambridge: Cambridge University Press, 1994), p. 168.

Chapter 8

1 *The Language Instinct* (London: Allen Lane, Penguin, 1994); quotes are from 2000 edn, p. 75.

2 *The Language of Thought* (Cambridge, Mass.: Harvard University Press, 1975).

3 Michael Devitt of the CUNY Graduate Center, quoted in the *New York Times*, 3 February 2001.

4 In 'The Life of Birds', presented by David Attenborough for the BBC Natural History Unit, 1998.

5 *The Language Instinct*, p. 55.

6 *Brainstorms: Philosophical Essays on Mind and Psychology* (London: Penguin, 1978); quote is from 1997 Penguin edn, pp. 101–2.

The duck-rabbit illustration is from J. Jastrow, *Fact and Fable in Psychology* (Boston: Houghton Mifflin, 1900). It was originally printed in the German humour magazine *Fliegende Blatter* (October, 1892).

Chapter 9

1 Maj. Gen. G. H. Israni, VSM, and Dr David R. Leffler, 'Operation: World Peace', *Defense India* (24 June 2002).

2 *Truth and Truthfulness* (Princeton and Oxford: Princeton University Press, 2002), p. 2.

3 Ibid., p. 8.

4 *Modernity and the Holocaust* (Oxford: Polity, 1979), p. 7.

5 Felix Guattari, *Chaosmosis: An Ethico-Aeshetic Paradigm*, trans. Paul Bains and Julian Pefanis (Bloomington: Indiana University Press, 1995), pp. 50–1.

6 Hugo Meynell, *Postmodernism and the New Enlightenment* (Washington, DC: The Catholic University of America Press, 1999), p. 178.

7 *Social Text* 46/47 (spring/summer 1996): 217–52.

8 For a full account and an amusing demolition of several key postmodern writers see Alan Sokal and Jean Bricmont, *Intellectual Impostures* (London: Profile, 1998).

9 *The Postmodern Condition: A Report on Knowledge* (Manchester: Manchester University Press, 1984), p. 60.

10 'Habermas and Lyotard on Post-Modernity', *Praxis*

International 4(1) (April 1984): 40.

11 'Pragmatism and Philosophy', in *Consequences of Pragmatism* (Minneapolis: University of Minnesota Press, 1982), introduction, 3 (i).

12 'Pragmatism, Davidson and Truth', in Ernest Lepore (ed.), *Truth and Interpretation* (Oxford: Blackwell, 1986), p. 351.

13 'Rational Animals', in Ernest LePore and Brian McLaughlin (eds), *Actions and Events* (Oxford: Blackwell, 1985), p. 480.

14 *Philosophy and Social Hope* (Harmondsworth: Penguin, 1999), p. 82.

15 Quoted in C. N. Degler, *In Search of Human Nature: The Decline and Revival of Darwinism in American Social Thought* (New York: Oxford University Press, 1991), p. 84.

16 *Philosophy and Social Hope*, p. 82.

17 'Pragmatism and Philosophy', in *Consequences of Pragmatism* (Minneapolis: University of Minnesota Press, 1982).

18 *Consequences of Pragmatism*, p. xxxvii.

19 *Scientific Autobiography and Other Papers*, trans. Frank Gaynor (New York: Greenwood 1968), pp. 33–4.

20 *Philosophy and Social Hope*, p. 37.

Chapter 10

1 Scribner, 2003. New York.

2 *Problems in Philosophy* (Oxford: Blackwell, 1993), pp. 3–4.

3 Ibid., p. 13.

4 Ibid., p. 4.

5 Ibid., p. 22.

6 Ibid., p. 154.

7 Ibid., p. 22.

8 'Does Consciousness Emerge from a Quantum Process?', *THES*, 5 April 1996.

9 'What is it Like to be a Bat?', in Douglas Hofstadter and Daniel C. Dennett (eds), *The Mind's I* (Harmondsworth: Penguin, 1982), pp. 394 and 396.

10 *Matters of Metaphysics* (Cambridge: Cambridge University Press, 1991), p. 9.

11 H. Dreyfus and S. Dreyfus, *From Socrates to Expert Systems: The Limits of Calculative Rationality* (1984). In Carl Mitcham and Alois Huning (eds), *Philosophy and Technology II: Information Technology and Computers in Theory and Practice*, Boston Studies in the Philosophy of Science Series (Reidel, 1985), pp. 111–130 (p. 113); available online at: <http://ist-socrates.berkeley. edu/ ~hdreyfus/html/paper_

socrates.html>.

12 Ibid.

13 *Problems in Philosophy*, p. 152.

Chapter 11

1 *Daily Telegraph*, 28 April 2004.

2 *Groundwork of the Metaphysic of Morals*, trans. H. J. Paton (New York: Harper and Row, 1964), section 1, para. 3.

3 In 'Moral Luck', *Mortal Questions* (Cambridge: Cambridge University Press, 1979), pp. 30–31.

4 In 'Moral Luck and the Virtues of Impure Agency', *Metaphilosophy* 22: 14–27.

5 'Luck and Desert', *Mind* 65 (1986): 198–209.

6 *The Therapy of Desire: Theory and Practice in Hellenistic Ethics* (Princeton: Princeton University Press, 1994), p. 96.

7 *Moral Luck: Philosophical Papers 1973-1980* (Cambridge: Cambridge University Press, 1981), p. 21.

8 Ibid., p. 39.

Chapter 12

1 David Niven, *The Moon's a Balloon* (London: Coronet, 1978), p. 217.

2 J. H. Burns and H. L. A. Hart (eds), *An Introduction to the Principles of Morals and Legislation* [1789] (London: Methuen, 1982); originally in John Bowring (ed.), *The Works of Jeremy Bentham*, 11 vols (Edinburgh, 1843), I, p. 143n.

3 'A Covenant for the Ark', *The Listener*, 14 April 1983.

4 Preface to 1975 edn of *Animal Liberation* (New York: New York Review of Books/Random House, 1975), p. ix.

5 'Armchair Moralising' (review of Peter Singer, *Writings on an Ethical Life*), *New Statesman*, 22 January 2001.

6 From 'Taking Life: The Embryo and the Fetus', in *Practical Ethics*, 2nd edn (Cambridge: Cambridge University Press, 1993), p. 153.

7 'Darwin for the Left', *Prospect* (June 1998).

Chapter 13

1 'Nothing Matters', in *Applications of Moral Philosophy* (London: Macmillan, 1972), pp. 37–8; extract available online at <http://www.hku.hk/philodep/courses/cvmol/HareMeaning.htm>.

2 *The Myth of Sisyphus*, trans. Justin O'Brien (Harmondsworth: Penguin, 2000), p. 109.

3 *In Good and Evil* (New York: Macmillan, 1970).

4 'Truth, Invention and the Meaning of Life', in *Needs,*

Values, Truth (Oxford: Blackwell, 1987), p. 91.

5 *Good and Evil*, p. 260.

6 'Truth, Invention and the Meaning of Life', in *Needs, Values, Truth* (Oxford: Blackwell, 1987), p. 91.

7 *How Are We to Live?* (London: Mandarin, 1994), pp. 206–7.

8 Ibid.

9 'The Meaning of Life', in E. D. Klemke (ed.), *The Meaning of Life* (Oxford: Oxford University Press, 1981), p. 128.

10 'The Meanings of the Question of Life', in *Paradox and Discovery* (Oxford: Blackwell, 1965), p. 40.

11 Ibid., p. 41.

12 *The Myth of Sisyphus*, trans. Justin O'Brien (New York: Vintage, 1960), pp. 3–4.

13 *Reasons and Persons* (Oxford: Oxford University Press, 1984), p. 175.

14 *The Doctor and the Soul* (New York: Alfred Knopf, 1957), p. 73.

15 'The Absurd', *Mortal Questions*, p. 11.

16 *Philosophical Explanations*, p. 585.

17 *Tractatus Logico-Philosophicus* 6.4312 (London: Routledge, 1993), p. 72.

18 A. W. Moore, *The Infinite* (London: Routledge, 1990), p. 227.

19 *The View From Nowhere* (Oxford: Oxford University Press, 1986), p. 224.

20 *Tractatus Logico-Philosophicus* 6.4311 (London: Routledge, 1993), p. 72.

index